formatio

TRADITION. EXPERIENCE.
TRANSFORMATION.

Formatio books from InterVarsity Press follow the rich tradition of the church in the journey of spiritual formation.
These books are not merely about being informed, but about
being transformed by Christ and conformed to his image.
Formatio stands in IVP's evangelical publishing tradition by
integrating God's Word with spiritual practice and by
prompting readers to move from inward change to outward
witness. IVP uses the chambered nautilus for Formatio, a
symbol of spiritual formation because of its continual spiral
journey outward as it moves from its center. We believe that
each of us is made with a deep desire to be in God's presence.
Formatio books help us to fulfill our deepest desires and to
become our true selves in light of God's grace.

Jane Rubietta

RESTING PLACE

A Personal Guide to Spiritual Retreats

IVP Books

An imprint of InterVarsity Press
Downers Grove, Illinois

InterVarsity Press
P.O. Box 1400, Downers Grove, IL 60515-1426
World Wide Web: www.ivpress.com
E-mail: mail@ivpress.com

InterVarsity Press® is the book-publishing division of InterVarsity Christian Fellowship/USA®, a student movement active on campus at hundreds of universities, colleges and schools of nursing in the United States of America, and a member movement of the International Fellowship of Evangelical Students. For information about local and regional activities, write Public Relations Dept., InterVarsity Christian Fellowship/USA, 6400 Schroeder Rd., P.O. Box 7895, Madison, WI 53707-7895, or visit the IVCF website at <www.intervarsity.org>.

All Scripture quotations, unless otherwise indicated, are taken from the Holy Bible, New International Version®. NIV®. Copyright ©1973, 1978, 1984 by International Bible Society. Used by permission of Zondervan Publishing House. All rights reserved.

Design: Cindy Kiple

Images: Mel Curtis/Getty Images

ISBN-10: 0-8308-3336-6
ISBN-13: 978-0-8308-3336-8

Printed in the United States of America ∞

Library of Congress Cataloging-in-Publication Data

Rubietta, Jane.
  Resting place: a personal guide to spiritual retreats / Jane
Rubietta.
    p. cm.
  Includes bibliographical references.
  ISBN 0-8308-3336-6 (pbk.: alk. paper)
  1. Spiritual retreats. 2. Spirituality. 3. Spiritual
life—Christianity. I. Title.
  BV5068.R4R83 2005
  269'.6—dc22

                                                 2005021332

P	19	18	17	16	15	14	13	12	11	10	9	8	7	6	5	4	3	2	1
Y	19	18	17	16	15	14	13	12	11	10	09	08	07	06	05				

With gratitude to my Shepherd, my Savior, my Resting Place,

for continually inviting me to find rest in him alone.

CONTENTS

INTRODUCTION

Water glides peacefully downstream, smoothing the river's edge, nibbling rocks away from their beds. No human feet have trampled the tall grasses and wildflowers along the bank; only a narrow trail created by thirsty deer and bear and other woodland animals breaks the growth undulating in the breeze.

Except—to the side a man stands beside a hammock, looking expectantly toward the hill. A feast spreads sumptuously across a woven blanket; a first-aid kit, a jug of water and a book of poetry complete the ensemble.

Sunlight drains from the sky; still he waits. Throughout the night, into the next day and the next, he waits.

He waits faithfully.

Finally footsteps pound on the nature trail, and he opens his arms. His face nearly breaks in half with his delight.

You rush past him. Your breath comes in gasps. You splash some water on your face, throw a smile in his direction and run back up the hill.

He resumes his position. Waiting. Waiting to cover your exhaustion with the warm blanket of his love, to offer absolute rest. Waiting to soothe the hot brow, rub ointment on blistered feet, pour water for the parched throat.

Waiting.

How long has it been since you met the Shepherd of your soul at the water's edge, since you took his arm and walked beside the tranquil waters, letting the beauty of his love and creation speak peace to your rattled soul? How long since you experienced more than a splash of cool water on your face, only to run off again in an endless race? More than a verse and a hurried prayer en route to the car or kids or daily commute?

King David really believed that the "Lord is my shepherd." His psalms often begin with him crying out to God for help, deliverance, revenge; David is stiff with anger or prostrate with pain or bent double with guilt. We read on to where he takes the Shepherd at his word, following him to still waters. Between the beginning and end of many of David's psalms is resolution. Problems aren't solved, but God restores his heart, refocuses his vision, soothes his pain.

The author of Psalm 23 seemed rational and accepting of rest, of God taking care of him, of the importance of soul restoration. David's present tense framing of the chapter points to his experience of life under the good Shepherd. Surely David wasn't an armchair theologian, a spoiled rich king living in a castle, never trusting these theories. He didn't just stroll about protected lawns and down to the stream, reclining for a bit while soldiers guarded him and women fed him grapes. Look at his life: David's family was messed up; people were always trying to kill him, even his closest relatives and friends; he connived and manipulated and just plain sinned. As king he reigned for many years, not on a throne but leading a ragtag bunch of fighters and stone throwers through wilderness and desert, sleeping in caves, running for their lives.

This concept of rest seems pivotal for a life of faith. Either God can take care of us or he isn't God—at least he's not a good God or an all-powerful God. Or maybe he's only the God of the good events and not God in the valley of the shadow, in the places that feel like death. He's only God when we feel goodness and mercy nipping at our heels, or feel the guiding staff, or when a banquet pops up in the middle of a battle with our enemies.

Maybe God isn't so good in a crisis, or God ducks out the back door at the first scent of trouble. Maybe we believe he's a good-time God, that the bill of goods we bought reads "Bad things only happen to people who don't trust God." We really believe God is the great Magician rather than the great Physician, and we shouldn't have "issues" once we know Jesus.

We *shouldn't* have problems with fatigue or depression or anger or control or abandonment. No dysfunction *should* ripple into our families. Our jobs *should* be advancing or at least stable and preparing us for retirement.

We *should* be bursting with love for everyone, be perfectly married or living joyfully though single. We *should* be living a victorious, effortless and powerful life.

Our "shoulds" and their accompanying guilt exhaust us. And I don't know a single person living like that. If I did, I wouldn't believe their assessment of their lives. Because bad things happen. This isn't heaven yet, as much as we'd like it to be. As much energy as we spend pretending that "it is well, it is well with my soul," is it really?

Probably not. A personal retreat allows us room to be honest with God about how imperfect we are, how disillusioned we are about our life and our inability to live holy and wholly this side of heaven.

THE PERSONAL RETREAT

Sixteen years ago, when I first began taking personal retreats—setting aside a day or two to be alone with God—I ran to God's arms for a day each month, fully aware of my flaws and sin. Each month I had to choose whether my problems with fatigue, emptiness, abandonment, balance, depression, anger, control, impotent Christianity and money would separate me from God and everyone I love, or lead me to God and to wholeness. As I continue to seek God in solitude, creativity and happiness, and the level of love in my relationship with God increase, so these subjects too are included.

The chapters in *Resting Place* allow us to unpack the baggage we haul around, using these issues as a starting point for our time with God, whether that is an overnight getaway or an afternoon alone in a quiet place. It is not necessary to read the chapters in order, but rather allow the Holy Spirit to highlight which subjects are important at this time to restore a resting heart.

A personal retreat is simply a concentrated and consecrated time with God. It is that resting place where we remove ourselves from the demands of our life and allow God to speak in an unhurried setting. Retreat centers scattered around North America work perfectly for the personal retreat, but a state park, a friend's empty home or some other setting works well, as long as solitude is possible and distractions minimal.

I don't run errands or check off a to-do list on a personal retreat, but I use specific tools that open my heart to God's presence and hush my soul. However, retreats aren't about running away from the world. They prepare us to love and serve those around us. Eventually, as God took me deeper into times of solitude, he also led me into a new ministry involving writing and speaking.

FOR YOUR RETREAT

The chapters include everything you need for a day away with the Shepherd. In each chapter you'll find the following tools that help us hear God's voice over our own bleating. Choose those that work best for you; a personal retreat needn't include every discipline mentioned.

Quotes to Contemplate

Hebrews 1:1 tells of the "great cloud of witnesses," and not long after rushing into the world on my own, I realized how badly I needed some witnesses to rise up and speak to me, guiding my journey toward wholeness. The quotes in this section are from soul models, either contemporary or classic, who have journeyed well and honestly, offering a guiding hand to steady our steps.

Meditate on Scripture

Scripture either validates or negates others' words, and God promises that his Word will not return empty. Here we interact with God's Word as it pertains to the chapter. One means of being with God through Scripture is an ancient method called *lectio divina* ("sacred reading," pronounced either lex-ee-oh or lek-tee-oh). This four-part process includes slow, measured reading and hearing of a verse or brief passage. Wait for a word or phrase or image to rise up from the reading, then move to meditating. Hold that before God. This deepening place and prayer allow God to expand it within and help us apply it. The stillness of contemplation follows, a silence that comes from being in God's presence. Over time, the stages of *lectio divina* become more natural, and Scripture becomes living and active.

⊗ *Journal Your Thoughts*

For centuries people have journaled to demonstrate their struggles and God's abounding love, power and presence. Psalms, Jeremiah, Lamentations and other portions of Scripture read like journals, reminding us that "The wisdom of the prudent is to give thought to their ways" (Proverbs 14:8). Regardless of journal type—handwritten or computer generated, spiral or hardback—the process becomes a type of detox, where we spill the contamination from living as imperfect people in an imperfect world; it serves as both confessional and prayer partner, offering accountability as we move through our days. This is not a legacy or keepsake to leave for others but a chronicle of our soul and God's work, and it charts our progress toward restoration.

⊗ *Respond in Prayer*

These include confession, praise, thanksgiving and petition, inviting God to search our hearts, cleanse us and set us free to praise and petition. Going boldly to his throne, we receive grace and find mercy.

⊗ *Consider Creation*

"The heavens declare the glory of God," but I get caught up in the things of this world and lose sight of the beauty around me. But beauty speaks of God's creative love for me, and on a personal retreat I delight in time alone in nature, even if it is observed through a window rather than experienced through a walk. God's genius and joy bloom in nature, and when I notice, I feel his love for me in new ways.

⊗ *Seek Stillness*

Henri Nouwen defined discipline as "the effort to create some space in which God can act. . . . It means somewhere you're not occupied, and you're certainly not preoccupied. It means to create that space in which something can happen that you hadn't planned on or counted on." Stillness and silence allow us to hear God and our own hearts, rather than the thumping of life run on the fast track. Here we settle in, shove aside words and give God our attention and our heart, inviting God to be present to us. Whether we hear direct words or he simply enfolds us in his love, this is a resting place that ultimately restores focus while renewing our hearts.

✍ *Reflection Questions*

Soul friends ask me caring but often hard questions, beckoning me into the catharsis of change and growth. They are application questions, requiring that I take stock of who I am, where I have come from, who I will be and how I will be different. In lieu of a personal visit from a friend or spiritual director, the questions in this section allow us room to apply what God seems to be pressing into our hearts.

✍ *Hymn of Praise*

Music reaches otherwise inaccessible parts of our soul. Music frees our spirit to embrace God in new ways, opening us to the presence of the Holy Spirit. Hymns, a rich tradition of Christian worship, become an integral part of restoration, of finding God as our resting place. Whether you can carry a tune or sound like a wooden bell when you sing, whether you sing them or read them aloud meditatively, the lyrics' depths allow God to speak to the soul.

✍ *Examen of Conscience*

Integrated in our personal retreat is the prayer of examen. This discipline is typically practiced at the end of a day, though it works at any time. Examen invites a twofold searching. Richard Foster calls these an "examen of consciousness," inviting God to search through our day with us to discover where we sensed or lost his presence; and an "examen of conscience," where we invite God to search our hearts for areas that need healing, purifying, cleansing.

FOR USE IN A SMALL GROUP

Resting Place is designed for individual and group use. Small groups may choose to slip away on retreat, using a chapter or two from the book as their guide. The tools in each chapter easily facilitate a small group meeting, allowing guidance for interaction as well as group contemplation and group *lectio divina*. Simply select a few of the disciplines and let the Holy Spirit facilitate the time together after discussion. Prayer and silence are life-giving in a group setting, and the hymns can be read slowly aloud as a group or as a form of meditation.

Resting Place is an invitation to journey through our fatigue to God's heart and into restoration. The book weaves together the issues that keep us from finding God as our resting place, the joys that emerge from that process and occasionally some thoughts from Psalm 23.

Is there a longing for deep rest buried under the chaos of daily life and work and play, the pressure of duties and commitments and oughts? Read, slowly, the words to Psalm 23.

> The LORD is my shepherd, I shall not want.
>> He makes me lie down in green pastures;
> he leads me beside quiet waters.
>> he restores my soul;
> He guides me in the paths of righteousness
>> for his name's sake.
> Even though I walk
>> through the valley of the shadow of death,
> I will fear no evil,
>> for you are with me;
> your rod and your staff,
>> they comfort me.
>
> You prepare a table before me
>> in the presence of my enemies.
> You anoint my head with oil;
>> my cup overflows.
> Surely goodness and love will follow me
>> all the days of my life,
> and I will dwell in the house of the LORD
>> forever.

Breathe deeply. What happened in your chest when you read those words, easing into them? What happened in your soul as you pictured the scene of restoration, of rejoicing?

The One who led David beside still waters waits for us to put our hand in his and to follow the overgrown path to the water's edge.

What keeps us from taking his outstretched hand? What will we gain—what will we lose—if we reach for him and hold on?

Come. Take a walk with me. And we will see.

1 ❧ RESTING PLACE

Discovering the Shepherd's Care

Well, God. Here I am. I feel crippled, as though coming through a debilitating accident, and I need extensive physical therapy in order to live well. Recovery means showing up at outpatient rehab repeatedly and allowing the therapist to work my muscles and lead me back to health.

It is odd to be in this place of breakdown—no, that's not the word—emotional and spiritual fatigue. Odd and fascinating as I consider the implications of living with you as my resting place. This may be the most important chapter of my life, right now, because you will, your Word will, teach me how to live, how to trust you, my Therapist, to rebuild my soul after an intensive season. Season? How about intensive life? The spiritual and emotional toll of these past few years is exorbitant.

Punching out from my waitress job, I rushed home to pack. Rich, my husband of seven months, worked the midnight shift at a shipping company, and when he returned at 2 a.m., we would load our gear for our first vacation as newlyweds, driving in the predawn hours to his family's cabin in the Northwoods.

Early in marriage we concurred that I am a horrible night passenger; I don't sleep in the car, and I steer the driver toward insanity with my questions: "Everything OK? You awake? Want me to drive?" My head bobs in sleepiness, but when the car sways around a curve, fear jerks me back to wakefulness and more distrustful and annoying queries.

So this night I drove our huge, ancient car, and Rich, nearly comatose from exhaustion, slept. We transferred seamlessly from Illinois interstate to Wisconsin road. The sun rose. Drowsiness crept over me, dulling my eyes. I tried tricks to stay awake. Chew each raisin fifteen times. Recite as much from the book of James as I could remember. Traffic picked up. Construction crews assembled, jackhammers pounded.

My head dipped. My eyes opened just in time to see the construction worker's terrified face as he dove behind a barricade, out of the way of our green tank.

My heart pounds remembering what could have been a tragic morning in many lives. How foolish to be driving without sleep, but I didn't question our prudence at all. I doubt I even awakened Rich to share the steering wheel. We were young, invincible and in a hurry. In a hurry to go on vacation. And rest.

FACTS ON FATIGUE

Fatigue is a fact of life. I recently said to Rich, nearly twenty-two years after that hurry-up-and-rest trip, "I don't want to wait for heaven to not be tired."

We are a tired society, even with an industry dedicated to leisure and its pursuit. We work hard, volunteer hard, buy expensive toys to play hard and sleep little. We exhaust our children by our efforts to provide them with an education and entertainment to rival our peers. We live with weariness as though it were expected and accepted and somehow spiritual.

WHAT'S THE BIG DEAL, THOUGH?

Rest serves a valid purpose in our lives. Sleep shucks off stress and its ill effects, refurbishes our bodies, repairs damage done during daylight hours, and rebuilds our endocrine and cardiovascular systems. Besides that, it feels good.

Rest seems like a good idea. David says, "He makes me lie down in green pastures, / he leads me beside quiet waters, / he restores my soul." But maybe rest was easier when David penned those lyrical phrases—in a world without electricity and flashlights and high-tech distractions like computers and beepers and wi-fi and twenty-four-hour news coverage. Maybe since they couldn't flip a switch and keep working, people got more sleep.

Maybe Psalm 23 was a public domain nursery rhyme. Everyone understood that day had limits and night was designed for sleeping, and of course God stood guard while you rested. Maybe rest was the default setting on their human software program.

Not likely. We have had choices from the beginning, when God created day and night, and then later when saying, "Six days you shall labor and do all your work" (Exodus 20:9), but on the seventh, "you must deny yourselves, and not do any work" (Leviticus 16:29).

Something is up, here, if God made rest mandatory. But this wasn't legalism. Rest communicates something basic about our relationship with God, and God's relationship with us.

AND THE VERDICT IS . . .

What am I trying to prove when I go without sleep? My answers sound defensive and flimsy: so much work, so little time, not enough help, too many people demanding pieces of me. Who will do the job if I don't?

We have always been tempted to overstretch our reach, to hyperextend, because Adam and Eve's affliction is ours as well: we want to be God. But why?

Because we don't trust God. Our fear factor kicks in when we consider going without work, when we contemplate actually viewing God as our Shepherd, who longs to lead us beside waters of rest, who eagerly anticipates restoring our soul, who wants nothing more than to have us lie down in green pastures. Fear looms larger, more real on the horizon of our mind than faith and reduces us to primal survival instincts: I must take care of myself; I'm my own bottom line. God doesn't love me, God won't care for me, God won't pick up the reins if I sleep. In fact, what if God really isn't God at all? I am the only one who has my best interests at heart.

Something happens between childhood's deep, trusting sleep and adulthood, when we shed youth's innocence and dress in robes of responsibility. On our own we move into sink-or-swim mode. Work becomes our life raft, our salvation. If we aren't working, we are not only worthless but in peril. No one comes along and shushes our fears with a gentle touch, swooping us onto a lap, rocking us to sleep, guarding our safety while we rest. Was this why Jesus said we needed to humble ourselves like little children and come to him (Mark 10:14-15)?

THE ENEMIES WILL EAT US: ENTERING THAT REST

When they drew back in terror at the edge of the Promised Land, the Israelites failed to enter God's rest (Numbers 14; Psalm 95:11), even after days of experiencing God's rescue, protection and provision. The Promised Land didn't contain much promise; it was a cruel ruse at the end of a long, harrowing trip.

They replied to God's invitation, "The land is filled with giants, and we will be like grasshoppers to them. They will eat us" (Numbers 13:33, my paraphrase).

We fail to enter God's rest when we refuse to trust and keep working, keep stirring the pot like the witches in Shakespeare's *MacBeth:* "Bubble, bubble, toil and trouble." Toil and trouble and lack of trust go hand in hand. When the Hebrew people chose to rest, to trust, they knew rest for their slaves, rest for their land, rest from war. Their lack of trust jeopardized their entire world—economic, physical, emotional and spiritual.

My work ethic muscles aside my wobbly-legged faith that God could care for me. But I do not want to live outside the Promised Land for the remainder of my life.

God said, "So don't fail to enter that rest—don't miss this!" (Hebrews 4:11, my paraphrase). Why return to our self-imposed slavery, to self-sufficiency?

This isn't feel-good theology. This is our Shepherd inviting us into rest—into renewal, into the meadow, rolling under the wind with its long multicolored grasses. He invites us to drop our bags and briefcases, take off our running shoes or wingtips, and stretch out beside the rippling stream of his loving care and protection and provision for us.

Our Shepherd invites us into a truly trusting relationship—not just on Sunday morning or at night—to test out whether God's promises are worth the paper they're printed on. If God "never slumbers or sleeps," then my exhaustion is unnecessary. I might as well put my head on God's shoulder and sleep.

What will we miss when we refuse those promises?

We will miss God. We will miss heaven on earth. We will miss the childlike delight of laying down our burdens and rolling down the hill outside our house.

The Promised Land—that land of rest—was not about heaven, someday when the roll is called up yonder. It was about daily life. It isn't that once inside the Promised Land, there would be no work, no worries, no wars. Rather, in the midst of those real-life problems, God would be present. God would care for his people and carry them, as in their wilderness passage. The burden would rest not on weary slave-shoulders but on God's. But they would not enter.

How like the Israelites we are. Years after the Promised Land U-turn, God says, "My people hath been lost sheep: their shepherds have caused them to go astray, they have turned them away on the mountains, . . . they have forgotten their restingplace" (Jeremiah 50:6 KJV).

Rather than leading us to God, our shepherds lead us astray. The project deadline, the toys in the floor or dishes in the sink, the weeds along the fence, the leaky pipe, the garage havoc, the big screen: these voices screech strident chords to us, demanding attention. The voices of our boss, our children, our spouse, our parents, our work ethic, our girlfriend or boyfriend: all compete for space in our busy brains.

But our deep cry echoes back centuries: "We are weary and find no rest" (Lamentations 5:5). It's time to pay attention to the cry in our heart for rest. We need our restingplace again.

There is only One.

RX FOR REST

Every morning this week, I awakened with a different song in my heart. One day it was Brahms' Lullaby. On another, it was my musician-husband's composition of Psalm 23. How beautiful of God to remind me at day's beginning that the day is more about resting in Christ than in working my list—to challenge me to carry that rest into the day.

Entering that rest—choosing God as our resting place—is more about our hearts and less about our hands. It's what is going on inside far more than what is going on outside. Rest is an internal state of soul, a relaxing into God's chest even when dashing through a day or a season. It has everything to do with whether we will allow God to shepherd us—feed and water us, rest us, restore us, guide us, protect us.

Rest helps us find meaning in our work and relationships, gives us places to evaluate what we're doing with our hours and our hearts, what difference it all makes. Rest—reflection, meditation, breathing in God's presence—lowers stress, calms our heartbeat and redirects our attention from the created to the Creator. Rest takes a load off.

We rest when we seek to live, work and sleep in Christ's presence. When we pursue God in solitude. We rest when we place our thoughts, loved ones, activities, emotions, efforts and ceaseless striving in God's hands. We rest when plans revolve around how much sleep we need, rather than working until we drop from exhaustion. We rest when we worship and praise, reaffirming Christ's lordship in our life and world.

This looks like turning to God in thanks, shifting from worry to gratitude or a few minutes of silence. Or in a moment of stillness inviting a word of Scripture to rise up from within. Or, like a runner in a marathon running hard but filled with oxygen, we rest when our heart is filled with God in the midst of our work.

Rest is a death. We die to ourselves, our agendas, and learn that God loves us deeply just as we are. We die to ourselves when we choose not to pummel God with more words but to simply sit as with a friend in silence, trusting the Spirit's words on our behalf. For even in our silence, the Holy Spirit intercedes for us, praying for us and through us.

This is the miracle: God's purposes may best be accomplished through our inactivity.

Our Shepherd holds out his hand and invites us to cease striving, to rest along the banks of still waters. And we lay down our knapsack, put our weary hand in his nail-scarred palm and let him lead us.

As you move into this respite, this retreat, may God be your resting place.

FOR YOUR RETREAT

Quotes to Contemplate

Contemplation is variously described as a "resting" in God or a "loving gaze" upon him or a "knowing beyond knowing" or a "rapt attention" to God. . . . To be a follower of Jesus, to be incorporated into him, and to receive his Spirit includes the potential of sharing in the contemplative experience. Indeed, in this sense it is our birthright as children of the same Father, and will become literally a lifeline of communication for his faith-filled follower.

THELMA HALL, *TOO DEEP FOR WORDS:*
REDISCOVERING LECTIO DIVINA

Blessed be to God for the day of rest and religious occupation wherein earthly things assume their true size. Ambition is stunted.

WILLIAM WILBERFORCE, QUOTED IN
GORDON MACDONALD, *ORDERING YOUR PRIVATE WORLD*

The person who establishes a block of time for Sabbath rest on a regular basis is most likely to keep all of life in proper perspective and remain free of burnout and breakdown.

GORDON MACDONALD, *ORDERING YOUR PRIVATE WORLD*

The indispensable condition for developing and maintaining the awareness of our belovedness is time alone with God. . . . Conscientiously "wasting" time with God enables me to speak and act from greater strength, to forgive rather than nurse the latest bruise to my wounded ego, to be capable of magnanimity during the petty moments of life. It empowers me to lose myself, at least temporarily, against a greater background than the tableau of my fears and insecurities, to merely be still and know that God is God.

BRENNAN MANNING, *ABBA'S CHILD*

In comparison with this big world, the human heart is only a small thing. Though the world is so large, it is utterly unable to satisfy this tiny heart. The ever-growing soul and its capacity can be satisfied only in the infinite God. As water is restless until it reaches its level, so the soul has not peace until it rests in God.

SUNDAR SINGH

Meditate on Scripture

God will speak to this people,
to whom he said,
    "This is the resting place, let the weary rest";
and, "This is the place of repose"—
    but they would not listen.
So then, the word of the LORD to them will become:
    Do and do, do and do,
rule on rule, rule on rule;
    a little here, a little there—
So that they will go and fall backward,
    be injured and snared and captured. (Isaiah 28:11-13)

My people hath been lost sheep: their shepherds have caused them to
go astray, they have turned them away on the mountains, they have
forgotten their restingplace. (Jeremiah 50:6 KJV)

I will refresh the weary and satisfy the faint. (Jeremiah 31:25)

Therefore, since we are surrounded by such a great cloud of witnesses,
let us throw off everything that hinders and the sin that so easily en-
tangles, and let us run with perseverance the race marked out for us.
Let us fix our eyes on Jesus, the author and perfecter of our faith, who
for the joy set before him endured the cross, scorning its shame, and
sat down at the right hand of the throne of God. Consider him who
endured such opposition from sinful men, so that you will not grow
weary and lose heart. (Hebrews 12:1-3)

[Moses said,] "If you are pleased with me, teach me your ways so I may
know you and continue to find favor with you." . . .
    The LORD replied, "My Presence will go with you, and I will give
you rest."
    Then Moses said to him, "If your Presence does not go with us, do
not send us up from here. How will anyone know that you are pleased
with me and with your people unless you go with us? What else will
distinguish me and your people from all the other people on the face
of the earth?" (Exodus 33:13-16)

When you lie down, you will not be afraid;
    when you lie down, your sleep will be sweet.
Have no fear of sudden disaster
    or of the ruin that overtakes the wicked,
for the LORD will be your confidence
    and will keep your foot from being snared. (Proverbs 3:24-26)

I will lie down and sleep in peace,

    for you alone, O LORD,

    make me dwell in safety. (Psalm 4:8)

Journal Your Thoughts

Write down your deepest protests about rest versus work. What part does fear play in any lack of rest? If God says, "you must deny yourself and do no work," what does a habit of exhaustion say about us? About our relationship with God?

Respond in Prayer

Turn your questions and fears into prayers of confession. Invite God into the process of moving from fear to faith, from work to rest, from exhaustion to restoring your soul.

Consider Creation

Where do you see principles of rest in creation? of trust? Ask God to transform those from principle to private truth as you seek to apply rest to your life, your lifestyle.

Seek Stillness

Try to remember the deepest, most restful sleep of your life. The Shepherd is inviting you to trust him and enter into a similar rest. Still your heart, your protests, and move there with him.

Reflection Questions

How much sleep do you get each night? When are your sleepiest times? Why do you go without enough rest, really? What keeps you awake at night?

Whose voices do you hear when you think about rest? What are they saying? To whose voice do you give the most credence: God's or someone else's? What drives you? Guilt? Work ethic? The party heart? What will keep you from finding God as your restingplace?

What are the ramifications of failure to rest? Consider health, relationships, priorities, God's calling. Do you believe this is a true equation: rest = trust? Evaluate how trust shows up in rest in your own life. When have you experienced a resting heart even while working?

What will your day look like when you plan it around resting with God and then working out of the overflow? How will you respond to the voices that clamor for attention to duty and responsibility?

In what small ways can you rest throughout the day?

Hymn of Praise

"Like a River Glorious"

Like a river glorious, is God's perfect peace,
Over all victorious in its bright increase;
Perfect, yet it floweth, fuller every day,
Perfect, yet it groweth deeper all the way.

Stayed upon Jehovah, hearts are fully blest,
Finding, as He promised, perfect peace and rest.

Hidden in the hollow of His blessed hand,
Never foe can follow, never traitor stand;
Not a surge of worry, not a shade of care,
Not a blast of hurry, touch the Spirit there.

FRANCES HAVERGAL, 1876

Examen of Conscience

Invite Christ to revisit your day with you. When did you sense God's presence? When did you rest, even while you kept moving? When did you lose the sense of "God with you"—Immanuel? Bring the events of the day to the Shepherd and let him carry you now, while you rest.

2 ❧ THE FAMISHED SOUL

Accepting God's Good Food

I like a full dishwasher, even when crammed with dirty dishes. It's satisfying because it shows that people have actually been eating at my house. Sometimes it is filled with bowls and spoons when I return from a trip. My family has been living on ice cream and canned soup in my absence. At least they get their minimum daily requirements of calcium through the ice cream, along with a week's worth of sodium in one can of soup.

Hunger. We open a fridge and say, "There's nothing to eat." When my children were little, they once came to me groaning. "My tummy hurts, Mommy." I looked at the clock. I had forgotten lunch. For the first time in their very short lives, they were acutely aware of hunger.

At birth, babies are gifted with a very clear mechanism for expressing need: they cry. Or scream. Or fuss. Or all three at the same time. This leaves the clever caregivers with the job of deducing the source of the cry. Is the baby's tummy empty or does the baby just need to be held?

At some point we are expected to grow up and figure out the source of our cry on our own time. No one can do this for us. Do we need to be held? Do we need to eat? How well we listen to our heart's cry determines much about the way we live. Hunger goes more deeply than an ache in our tummy.

How aware are we of our own hunger now? Of its disguises, and what it really means?

Consumed with Hunger

Huge golden-orange koi stocked the stream. Near the bridge, where tourists stood with fish snacks, the koi gathered. They vied for surface space, tussling about, pushing to the top, mouths open in a grotesque sucking position as they tried snagging the next crumbs.

Like the koi, hunger consumes us, or at least food and its consequences and companions consume us. Books on exercise, diet and food glut the bookshelves. Two-thirds of American adults are overweight or obese, as well as thirty-some percent of children ages six to nineteen, according to research. Anorexia and bulimia run rampant in our society. Small wonder weight loss is big business, with dietary supplements, dietary experts and diets to fit every possible compulsion and problem. Mirrors line workout worlds, and gyms bulge with people wanting to become more acceptable according to the world's definition of beauty.

The pace of our days feeds the problem: the minivan substitutes for the kitchen, and we fast-food our way through life. Women average one meal a day, nibbling around their remaining nutritional needs, ambushing their metabolism. We watch our cholesterol, count carbs and somehow believe that what we see is who we are.

Who we are is a society of starved souls. Our hunger is a soul issue. We become spiritual anorexics hopping from one church to another, one gimmick to another, trying to find some kind of convenience food for the soul in hopes of alleviating surface hunger pains. To assuage the hunger, we join committees, do more work, never realizing that without deep soul food our good works leech the marrow from our bones. Like the prodigal son, we attempt to fill ourselves with husks from the pigpen rather than riches from the Father's table. We cram our lives with people and possessions but let others determine our priorities.

We have it backward. Our being must precede our doing and consuming if we are to grow up into all the fullness of Christ. As Ruth Senter writes, when we are weary and vulnerable, looking for ways to feed our souls, God's desire is clear:

You want to know how to motivate others to do love? It isn't by doing more love so you can be their model. It's by coming close to Me, letting My love soak into you like water saturating a sponge. Others will know when you are full. When their lives touch yours, love will seep out. Then it will be My love that motivates them, not your deeds. . . . As you drink deeply of My love, you will be strengthened and renewed. Then the doing of your love will be the overflow. . . . You must *be* my love before you can *do* my love. Perhaps it is the greater side of faith for you to say, "I love You, Lord," and not do anything.

Our appetite hides—or perhaps reveals—our heart.

SYMPTOMS OF SOUL HUNGER

A TV commercial asked, "What do you want when you don't know what you're hungry for?" The American answer is a candy bar, stashed in a purse or a desk drawer, a quick pick-me-up full of nothing good for us except a few peanuts buried in half a day's worth of empty calories.

Most of us don't know what we're hungry for, so we try to fill up with something, anything that appeases.

A manufacturer's jingle from my childhood asked, "How do you handle a hungry man?" Naturally, with a can of brawny meat, sure to win the little woman a place in the man's heart. The assumption is that food will solve our need for attention and love.

Proverbs 27:7 says, "He who is full loathes honey, / but to the hungry even what is bitter tastes sweet." When we do not sate our hunger appropriately, we blindly attempt to nourish our longing with what is bitter.

Food is not the only way we try to soothe the beast; we also attempt to nurture this starved soul through excessive emotions, activities and behaviors. Our hungry heart expresses itself profoundly through our emotions or the anesthetizing of them. The hollow core of our souls is easily, though temporarily, fooled by substances and activities that promise satisfaction but create a deeper longing.

"We are diminished by the trivial things we treasure," wrote John of the Cross. "You are what you love." This is not good news. Not unless we are willing to take stock of our treasure trove and listen to our soul's cry.

When are you very, very still, what do you hunger for?

TRUE FAMINE AND DEEP HUNGER

Our hunger emanates from a deeply seeded, Eden-originated longing. "What a man desires is unfailing love" (Proverbs 19:22). We were made for love. For an unending, uncompromising, unconditional type of love. Excessive emotions, activities and behaviors are futile attempts to plug a hole designed to be filled by God alone.

> "The days are coming," declares the Sovereign LORD,
>   "when I will send a famine through the land—
> not a famine of food or a thirst for water,
>   but a famine of hearing the words of the LORD." (Amos 8:11)

We long for the soothing Shepherd's call of love, of protection, of mercy and presence.

And God is calling us to the dinner table.

> He is wooing you from the jaws of distress
>   to a spacious place free from restriction,
>   to the comfort of your table laden with choice food. (Job 36:16)

TIME TO EAT

Hunger's outworking shows up spiritually. Do we confuse ministry with meat? Jesus said, "My food is to do the will of him who sent me" (John 4:34), and we emphasize the "to do," writing it at the top of our list. But Jesus continually fed his heart on God's presence. He so delighted in God that he disciplined himself to live in unbroken communion with God, as though a continuous IV dripped into his soul as he went about life on earth. Solitude further prepared Jesus to accomplish his purpose—doing the will of "him who sent me."

But we don't notice the IV; we see Jesus busy about the Father's work and figure we too must busy ourselves with the work of the kingdom. We disconnect the IV and run about, never recognizing the slow starvation of our soul, wishing only for applause from the spectators lining the sides of our lives.

Constant activity—even good ministry activity—cannibalizes our soul. In Mark 6:30-31, after dramatic missionary travels, Jesus' disciples returned, thrilled over miracles accomplished in Jesus' name. "The apostles gathered around Jesus and reported to him all they had done and taught. Then, because so many people were coming and going that they did not even have time to eat, he said to them, 'Come with me by yourselves to a quiet place and get some rest.' "

But noisy people followed them to that quiet place, the day slipped away, and the hot dog stand at the nearby stadium closed. So the disciples, who hadn't had time to eat before this jaunt out to the solitude of a thousand people, were exhausted with emptiness and expected Jesus to take care of his disciples' needs. They asked Jesus about sending the hoards away to find some food on their own. "You give them something to eat," Jesus answered (Mark 6:37).

The disciples couldn't feed the crowd. They couldn't even feed themselves. But Jesus could. That is the whole point.

FILLING

Like old Mother Hubbard exploring her neighbor's cupboard, I search the Scriptures in my hunger. *Filling* and *fill* appear multiple times. The Word promises that we will be filled with the Holy Spirit, filled with wisdom, filled with joy, with all knowledge, with comfort. "Blessed *are you* who hunger now, / For you shall be filled" (Luke 6:21 NKJV). *Filled* in this passage leans toward supplying food in abundance, from the word for "gorge." This does not sound like starvation rations or pods from the pigsty; and hope nourishes.

The gospel of Luke opens with the statement "He has filled *the* hungry with good things" (1:53 NKJV). In the original, translated here as "filled," the word means "satisfy," but a deeper look traces its ancestry to the word *rest*. This word is rarely used with verbs of motion and indicates a fixed position. This filling is somehow related to resting. God is gracious, promising filling for the hungry soul—filling that comes not by striving but by resting.

We expend such energy, trying to satisfy a hunger that God promises to fill. Jesus tells us: "So do not worry, saying, 'What shall we eat?' or 'What shall we drink?' . . . For the pagans run after all these things, and your heavenly Father knows that you need them" (Matthew 6:31-32). Not only will God satisfy our physical hunger by providing literal food, but our spiritual gauntness will be satisfied by Jesus; it can only be filled by the One who said, "I am the bread of life" and "the one who feeds on me will live because of me" (John 6:35, 57).

Isn't that what we really crave? Life.

A BANQUET

A pheasant sits in the backyard on newly mown fall grass, pecking at something. A leaf? A milkweed pod? There is nothing relaxed, however, about the bird's eating. A vigilant eye watches for predators. Unless a fox or coyote appears, the bird is safe. But he doesn't know safety in his bird life or bird brain, and he cannot leisurely enjoy his seed-pod supper.

God shows how to dine. "You prepare a table before me under the eyes of my enemies . . . my cup brims over" (Psalm 23:5 NJB). This is true hospitality to the hungry, wandering heart. The Shepherd invites us to step aside from mindless, sheeplike wandering, from our fear-filled rushing, from all our excessive living and to recline at the table with him. Imagine: the enemies are approaching—perhaps the internal demons that always want to pull the meat from the bones of our soul, or perhaps the external howling demands that are impossible to satisfy, the career expectations, endless rounds of to-dos, unending duties. Countless obligations jam our brain and cry for attention.

The Shepherd meets us at the gate, presses a cool cloth over our forehead, kisses our cheek, washes our feet and bids us sit. Recline. Let him serve us.

So we heed the cry of our soul and the invitation of our Shepherd, and we move toward that banquet that is his loving, unending presence. Our hunger keeps us moving and consuming, preventing us from truly resting. When we learn to feast on God's presence, our appetite for false food loses its power. Whether we feast through silence, through stillness, through meditation or contemplation, God longs to feed us.

And he leads us beside a rippling stream, where a table gleams with white linen and platters groan with delicacies. Seating us, spreading a napkin over our lap, he stands guard, holding off the enemies braying for our heart and soul. We dine in this sanctuary.

As you prepare to feast, may God become, again, your resting place.

FOR YOUR RETREAT

Quotes to Contemplate

The point is this: I saw more clearly than ever, that the first great and primary business to which I ought to attend every day was to have my soul happy in the Lord. The first thing to be concerned about was not how much I might serve the Lord, how I might glorify the Lord; but how I might get my soul into a happy state, and how my inner man might be nourished. . . . The first thing the child of God has to do morning by morning is to obtain food for his inner man.

As the outward man is not fit for work for any length of time except if we take food, and this is one of the first things we do in the morning, so it should be with the inner man. Now what is the food for the inner man? Not prayer, but the word of God; and here again not the simple reading of the word of God, so that it only passes through our minds, just as water runs through a pipe, but considering what we read, pondering over it, and applying it to our hearts.

GEORGE MUELLER, *SOUL NOURISHMENT FIRST*

[Jesus said], "Blessed are they which do hunger and thirst after righteousness, for they shall be filled." Aching, longing, hungering, and thirsting are the signals by which our authentic selves call us toward our

destiny. *Every destructive or "bad" desire is a substitute for the constructive longing of the true self. . . . Every single person I'd interviewed was using his or her particular habit as a substitute for good emotional health, specifically the ability to give and receive love. Though these addicts' ways of trying to fulfill their desires were extremely dysfunctional, their real desires were not only natural, but essential. . . .*

Eating is such a simple, reliable comfort that if we don't care for our souls, it's very easy to get in the habit of using food to distract ourselves from pain that has nothing to do with physical appetite.

MARTHA BECK, THE JOY DIET

> *Those of us who walk along this road*
> *do so reluctantly. . . .*
> *We'd rather be more active—*
> *planning and scurrying around.*
> *All this is too contemplative to suit us.*
> *Besides we don't know what to do*
> *with piousness and prayer.*
> *Perhaps we're afraid to have time to think,*
> *for thoughts come unbidden.*
> *Perhaps we're afraid to face our future*
> *knowing our past.*
> *Give us the courage, O God,*
> *to hear your word*
> *and to read our living into it.*
> *Give us the trust to know we're forgiven,*
> *and give us the faith*
> *to take up our lives and walk.*

ANN WEEMS, KNEELING IN JERUSALEM

We don't live by bread alone, but we also don't live long without it. To eat is to acknowledge our dependence—both on food and on each other. It also reminds us of other kinds of emptiness that not even the blue-plate special can touch.

FREDERICK BUECHNER, *BEYOND WORDS*

My lack of tears worried, then frightened me.

So I began to study other men and was comforted to find I was not alone. . . . I could feel the tears within me, undiscovered and untouched in their inland sea. Those tears had been with me always. I thought that, at birth, American men are allotted just as many tears as American women. But because we are forbidden to shed them, we die long before women do, with our hearts exploding or our blood pressure rising or our livers eaten away by alcohol because that lake of grief inside us has no outlet. We, men, die because our faces were not watered enough.

PAT CONROY, *BEACH MUSIC*

Meditate on Scripture

I tell you the truth, you are looking for me, not because you saw miraculous signs but because you ate the loaves and had your fill. Do not work for food that spoils, but for food that endures to eternal life, which the Son of Man will give you. . . .

I am the bread of life. He who comes to me will never go hungry, and he who believes in me will never be thirsty. (John 6:26-27, 35)

Open wide your mouth and I will fill it. . . .
But you would be fed with the finest of wheat;
    with honey from the rock I would satisfy you. (Psalm 81:10, 16)

And the Word became flesh, and dwelt among us, and we saw His glory, glory as of the only begotten from the Father, full of grace and truth. . . . For of His fullness we have all received, and grace upon grace. (John 1:14, 16 NASB)

O GOD, You are my God; I shall seek You earnestly;
My soul thirsts for You, my flesh yearns for You,
In a dry and weary land where there is no water.
Thus I have seen You in the sanctuary,
To see Your power and Your glory.
Because Thy lovingkindness is better than life,
My lips will praise You.
So I will bless You as long as I live;
I will lift up my hands in Your name.
My soul is satisfied as with marrow and fatness,
And my mouth offers praises with joyful lips. (Psalm 63:1-5 NASB)

He humbled you, causing you to hunger and then feeding you with manna, which neither you nor your fathers had known, to teach you that man does not live on bread alone but on every word that comes from the mouth of the LORD. (Deuteronomy 8:3)

Your love, O LORD, reaches to the heavens,
your faithfulness to the skies.
Your righteousness is like the mighty mountains, . . .
How priceless is your unfailing love!
Both high and low among men
find refuge in the shadow of your wings.
They feast on the abundance of your house;
you give them drink from your river of delights.
For with you is the fountain of life;
in your light we see light. (Psalm 36:5, 7-9)

Journal Your Thoughts

Consider your excessive emotions, activities, behaviors. Begin to dump out your thoughts about hunger, any fear about having your needs met or being disappointed in those places where disapproval or pain met the longing for love. Pour this out to God and turn it into prayer.

Respond in Prayer

Ask God to bring any sin to mind, and experience the clean sweep of repentance and forgiveness. Move into adoration, thanksgiving and petition. Invite God to fill your hungry heart.

Consider Creation

Look around with the companionship of the Lord of the harvest. Where do you see examples of God's faithfulness, principles of hunger and feeding, of God's care of creation? "Look at the birds of the air; they do not sow or reap or store away in barns, and yet your heavenly Father feeds them. Are you not much more valuable than they?" (Matthew 6:26)

Seek Stillness

Ask God to settle your soul, to shush the striving and straining of the day past or the day to come. Invite the Holy Spirit to help you locate your deepest hunger. Allow the longing of your heart to rise. Place that hunger into Jesus' hands. Imagine him, the Shepherd of your soul, receiving that gift and filling you with his presence, his unfailing love.

Reflection Questions

How is your hunger displayed? Where does your hunger, your longing lead you? Now wait with that manifestation: shop, eat, rage, sleep, a new car, decorations, fast food, a new job, a child, a spouse, healing. Invite God into that longing.

Imagine yourself as a baby, either needing to be held or fed. When were you fed when you were really longing to be held? How do you carry that longing into life now?

What is the root of your hunger? When are you most susceptible to that manifestation? How do you circumvent that, getting your hunger to lead you to God?

When have you hurt others by the way you attempted to satiate your hunger? When have you hurt yourself? What do you need to do to make amends?

How have you found God's filling? What works in the midst of the cry of your soul?

Hymn of Praise

"O Food to Pilgrims Given"

Chorus:
Whom have I in heav'n but you?
And earth has nothing I desire besides you.
My heart and flesh may fail,
But God is the strength of my heart.
God is my portion for ever.

O food to pilgrims given,
O bread of life from Heaven,
O manna from on high!
We hunger, Lord supply us,
Nor thy delights deny us,
Whose hearts to thee draw nigh.

O stream of love past telling,
O purest fountain, welling
From out the Savior's side!
We faint with thirst; revive us,
Of thine abundance give us,
And all we need provide.

O Jesus, by thee bidden,
We here adore thee, hidden
In forms of bread and wine.
Grant when the veil is riven,
We may behold, in heaven,
Thy countenance divine.

MAINTZICH GESANGBUCH, 1661; TRANS. JOHN ATHELSTAN RILEY, 1906

Examen of Conscience

Scroll through your day with Jesus' hand in yours. Where did you react in a way that now makes you think you were longing for love? Where did your appetite get confused with your hunger for God's presence? Allow the Comforter to come, soothe, be present to you and guide you into fullness of joy.

3 ❧ ABANDONMENT AND GOD

Finding Safety in Relationships

The road narrowed and the terrain rose, sure signs we neared the cabin in Michigan's Upper Peninsula. I topped a hill, Rich in the passenger seat and the children strapped in the back. Looking toward oncoming traffic, I pointed to the left shoulder of the road. "What's that? A pile of dirt?" As we drew nearer, I gasped. "It's a bear! It's been hit!"

We pulled over. Rich checked the bear, then beckoned us to join him. The children clambered out. I gritted my teeth and crossed my arms over my chest as if holding my heart in place. My face in the rearview mirror grew pale and strained.

Other cars stopped, drivers gawked, crowds gathered. In the Upper Peninsula, bears thunder through forests carefree and unrestrained; but a bear stretched across the roadside was unusual. My shaking did not quell. Unable to sit still with myself any longer, I eased out of the car.

A vehicle had struck the bear in the hip. A bullet hole, no doubt to end her pain, pierced her furry chest. Her teats, exposed to the world, revealed her status as a nursing mother. The vulnerability of that pink flesh surrounded by coarse dark fur hurt me. In directing traffic for her cubs, she got them across the highway but gave up her life in the end.

The image of the cubs, confused in the woods, gripped me. How would they live without their mama to show them the way? Horror at the abandonment, the senseless death, blurred my eyes. Sobs climbed in my throat.

Blinking, I pulled my own cubs from the death scene, containing my emotions until I could examine them without traumatizing the children.

DESERTED BY LOVE

This physiological reaction to the bear graphically illustrated my fear of abandonment. To avoid that I kept relationships shallow and therefore safe. In college I dated broadly and usually briefly. Once, when I showed up at home on a break, my mother asked about a recent beau. I shrugged. Her next words convicted me: "What are you afraid of?"

"To be deserted by love," writes Ruth Senter, "is quite possibly the worst torture of the soul." Who wants to be like those cubs, left alone with no one to love them or teach them to hunt, to fish or to save their own lives? We may protect ourselves in relationships as if afraid of abandonment or rejection. We become relational misers. In our flimsy tenements—these flesh-and-blood buildings—we have no truly sheltering, enduring relationships. Maybe we hesitate to get wrapped up in marriage because, well, it might not be a forever deal.

Relationships on earth offer no guarantees. And this is right. Perhaps we all need to experience abandonment at some point, so we learn to seek permanence and fulfillment in the right place: in God rather than others. Unless identified and resolved, abandonment issues will keep us from trusting our Shepherd, from following him into places of rest.

LONGING FOR NEVER-LEAVING LOVE

Nestled into abandonment is a discomfort with who we are, a composite of gifts and defects. Have we truly experienced another's never-leaving love at our worst and most broken? Not wanting to see ourselves as that broken-down soul with no merit, desperately needing a Savior—helpless cubs alone in the woods—our internal accommodator kicks in. We puff and pretend and get busy, work hard and try to secure relationships with a perfect façade. We defend our rightness, bluff, brag, argue, determine to win at any cost. Or we underachieve so we don't have to disappoint ourselves or others. This way, we abandon our true self before anyone can leave us.

Rolling the film of our lives backward, it may halt at our deepest wound—a wound inflicted, perhaps unintentionally, when someone we loved did not act lovingly toward us or left us in the lurch. From that point forward, does the film portray our self-defense from such vulnerability? A vulnerability rooted in fear that we are not worth loving, and desertion will be our reward for our defectiveness.

Many people spend the rest of their lives living out of that fear, prickly and angry or overly helpful, or with a string of broken engagements or marriages like hubcaps along the roadside. "No one will ever really love me, so I will cut the line first," we reason. Or we never engage in the first place. We hold ourselves back, afraid we will fail or others will fail us, or we won't be able to "love without end, amen" and thus will not merit love in return.

We protect our heart from ever being hurt again.

PHYSICAL ABANDONMENT

Diane's father died when she was three. For months she cried through the night, insisting on a light. Her soft soul interpreted her father's death as abandonment. When her stepfather showed up, rough and abusive, her sense of safety shrank, and she was shipped off to live with relatives. After marriage, Diane's fear of abandonment muzzled her family. If her husband was one minute late coming home from work, she fretted that he'd died in an accident. As her children grew, Diane loosened her hold but panic still gripped her heart. What if they walked away and never came back? What if their relationship changed permanently?

Physical abandonment issues plague all stratum of our society and church. The absentee parent, the workaholic spouse, the rich suburban coed with money to burn and no one around to curtail the craziness with loving presence: these behaviors are hidden in the carefully made-up smiles of our pew people as well. The college student who dates wildly in an effort to get attention, single parent families, foster children shuffled from house to house in search of a home: abandonment issues may appear in all these hearts as the accommodator whispers, "See, no one really loves you. No one will stay."

EMOTIONAL ABANDONMENT

Emotional abandonment begins in childhood, and children carry their emotional abandonment to class. So Rob, a teacher, tries not to be absent, because children need consistency. Once, when Rob returned from a sick day, little George took one look at him and turned his back. "You weren't here," he accused, and wouldn't talk to him all day.

My fear of abandonment appears as withdrawing: an unwillingness to be open, lack of eye contact or spontaneous sharing or laughter or touching. It keeps me from resolving conflict, asking hard questions, setting personal boundaries or limits on our children.

Drew won sales awards in his field and worked long hours, rarely seeing his family. His wound began when he himself toddled about, looking for his daddy's heart. The father finally showed up, wanting to begin a similar business in a far-distant town. Drew so hungered for his father's never-leaving love that he abandoned his family and moved away to start a business with long-lost Dad. The cycle of abandonment began again, with his cast-off family.

We make choices that perpetuate our abandonment fears. A classic example happens in families of alcoholics, but the truth transfers to all children of abandonment—to all of us to some degree. As the children grow up:

> We either become alcoholics, marry them, or both, or find another compulsive personality to fulfill our sick abandonment needs. . . . We are dependent personalities who are terrified of abandonment and will do anything to hold onto a relationship in order to not experience painful abandonment feelings which we received from living with . . . people who were never there emotionally for us.

SPIRITUAL ABANDONMENT

Physical and emotional abandonment lead into spiritual abandonment. The abandoned heart subconsciously interprets others' behaviors as a reflection on God. If a tangible, breathing, flesh-and-blood parent can forsake us, what about an invisible heavenly parent? If a soul friend, who has shared our deep secrets and challenges, can desert us, how do we sing "What a Friend We Have in Jesus" when we can't touch this Jesus friend?

We find ourselves alone in brokenness, questioning God: "Why did you leave? Where were you? Why did you allow that tragedy?" The abandoned child concludes: "God doesn't love me. God isn't good. God isn't real."

But at other points we experience John of the Cross's "dark night of the soul." We trust God but don't sense God's presence. Whether battling unanswered prayer or God's silence or a seeming aloneness, suffering feels like punishment. The psalmist cries, "How long, O LORD? Will you forget me forever? / How long will you hide your face from me?" (Psalm 13:1).

God's hiddenness can be expected, even embraced, as part of the prayer experience. His seeming distance does not necessarily indicate God's displeasure or our sin. This sense of God's absence is actually grace disguised.

How tempting it is to make God into our own likeness, to reduce this Creator of the universe to a formula, someone who comes running when I whimper, jumps when I call, answers all my list prayers, does what I want. In *Ascent of Mount Carmel,* John of the Cross writes:

> When some of this solid, perfect food (the annihilation of all sweetness in God—the pure spiritual cross and nakedness of Christ's poverty of spirit) is offered them in dryness, distaste, and trial, they run from it as from death and wander about in search only of sweetness and delightful communications from God. Such an attitude is not the hallmark of self-denial and nakedness of spirit but the indication of a spiritual sweet tooth.

God's seeming absence is not abandonment. Perhaps in the dark God asks, "Will you abandon me though you cannot feel me, see me, touch me? Can I be who I am and still have you love me? Will you trust me in the night-time?" Isn't this the deepest cry of our own soul, the cry that wrenches from our gut in places of our own wounding? And won't God bring us to the place where we are forced to choose to stay, in spite of the darkness?

THE NEED FOR ABANDONMENT

Deep weariness may accompany abandonment fear, an aching that comes from creation, a crying out for God. When our hearts ache, "Why have you left? Don't you love me?" we move into alignment with Jesus. Our cries are a whisper of his voice on the cross, "My God, my God, why hast Thou forsaken me?" Without his forsakenness, we would not know never-leaving love. We would be abandoned in our brokenness, broken in our longing for love, orphaned on the shoulder of life.

But because of our brokenness Christ was forsaken, abandoning forever all possibilities of our abandonment, separation, from God. Because of Christ's forsakenness, we can live in never-leaving love.

God has said,
> "Never will I leave you;
> never will I forsake you."

So we say with confidence,
> "The Lord is my helper; I will not be afraid.
> What can man do to me?" (Hebrews 13:5-6)

CHOOSING ABANDONMENT, CHOOSING ABANDON

As children, we could not choose our living situation or the circumstances or people creating or contributing to our wounds. We didn't know how to contradict seeming messages of abandonment.

Now, as adults, we can choose to believe the internal accommodator, who whispers various instructions: "Shape up! Perform. Work hard. Don't trust. Run away. No one will love you. Pretend." We can choose to believe that we are unacceptable and abandoned, and then live in that wound.

Or we can choose to believe God's words about us, who planned us from time's birth, wove us in our mother's womb, loves us forever. Loves us with our bed head and whiskers. Delights in us without our makeup or when the scales reveal our late-night refrigerator raids. Doesn't put stipulations on our dates ("I will love you if . . .") or how clean the car is, or our bank balance or anything else the world grades us on or pretend loves us for.

"I will betroth you to me forever;
  I will betroth you in righteousness and justice,
    in love and compassion
I will betroth you in faithfulness." (Hosea 2:19-21)

We deny the abandonment lies. In our anti-abandonment campaign, we refute the rules ordering us to not trust, not love, not touch or we will be hurt. We choose to not interpret others' behavior as a reflection of our lack of worth but as a display of their own woundings.

This is not denial. We aren't invincible and invulnerable. We don't—can't—feign cheerfulness in the midst of pain. Rather, we acknowledge the hurt, feel it, and then can say, "That hurt me. But that's not who you really are." Though wounded by others' wounds, we can call out their best. We also respect the soft spot of our soul by choosing safe relationships, places that honor the need for nurture and love.

We can abandon our own abandonment behavior.

And we learn to live with abandon, in two senses. One, that abandonment is inevitable: people will fall short of our need to be totally safe in relationship. Two, we can learn to live freely, to abandon our wounds, our needs to please and our feelings of worthlessness.

LIVING WITH ABANDON

As a verb, *abandonment* means to surrender power. The noun describes an enthusiasm, exuberance or unconstraint. *Abandoned* can mean given up, forsaken or wholly free from restraint.

Christ's never-leaving love changes everything: how we awaken in the morning, how we treat the phone solicitor or the spouse who forgets something vital to us, how we love. As we learn to live with our own imperfections and not abandon our true self, we will interpret others' behaviors and attitudes as examples of their abandonment fears and their need for never-leaving love.

This abandonment moves us into the abundant life Christ offers (John 10:10). Because for the first time, we are living in freedom unrelated to others' real or imagined feelings about us, a freedom totally related to God. A reckless ability to love fills us, a love that says, "I'm here. I'm not leaving. And I'm not abandoning my own heart! I'm going to love, no matter what." And abandon begins. Joy perks, bubbles over. We laugh and smile and grow up into all the fullness of Christ as we embrace our brokenness, find ourselves complete in Christ and fill our tanks with his never-leaving love.

Once, when we were playing as children, my brother bit me. He didn't even break the skin, but I was so outraged at the injury that I had to show my father. The only problem was, Dad wouldn't be home for hours—and by then, my wound would be invisible. So I rebit myself repeatedly throughout the day, because I wanted justice and attention.

Living with abandon means to abandon our tendency to freshen and nurse our wounds. We abandon the right to hold grudges and withhold forgiveness. This abandonment sets us free.

A LEADING LOVE

Our Lover invites us to trust, to rest beside still waters, to succumb to his protection and provision. When abandonment fear kicks in, acknowledge, then quiet the internal accommodator who reads old cue cards from offstage, "Work. Harder. Don't stop. Don't trust. Don't touch." Let abandonment fear move you back into the never-leaving love of God, where soul-hushing begins. The Shepherd soothes us, smoothing our hair, holding us against his chest, and we begin to relax, to lean into that love.

May Christ be your resting place as you heed your soul cry for the complete, never-leaving love of our Shepherd and Savior.

FOR YOUR RETREAT

Quotes to Contemplate

Gracious God,
make me sensitive to all
the evidences of your goodness;
and may I, trusting in you,
free myself of the terror of death,
and feel free to live intensely and happily
the life you have given me. Amen.

RUBEN ALVES, *I BELIEVE IN THE RESURRECTION OF THE BODY*

Every man God has used first suffered adversity and seeming
abandonment. Think of Jacob, running from Esau's death threats; Joseph,
sold into slavery and unjustly imprisoned; Moses, fleeing Pharaoh's palace
to tend sheep for 40 years; or King David, hiding from Saul's jealous rages.
Yahweh deals with our pride and self-sufficiency through adversity. . . .
In adversity our intellectual knowledge becomes actual knowledge.

LYNN N. AUSTIN, *MY FATHER'S GOD*

God, of your goodness give me yourself;
for you are sufficient for me.

I cannot properly ask anything less,
to be worthy of you.
If I were to ask less, I should always be in want.
In you alone do I have all. Amen.

JULIAN OF NORWICH, ENGLAND, FIFTEENTH CENTURY

Attachment, or bondedness, is our deepest need . . . because it is also the
deepest part of the character of God. . . . Repairing bonding deficits
involves two factors. First, it requires finding safe, warm relationships in
which emotional needs will be accepted and loved, not criticized and
judged. . . . Second, repair requires taking risks with our needs. It means
bringing our loneliness and abandoned feelings to other believers in the
same way Jesus revealed in the Beatitudes: "Blessed are the poor in spirit,
for theirs is the kingdom of heaven. Blessed are those who mourn, for they
shall be comforted" (Matt. 5:3-4 NASB).

These are genuine risks. No matter how safe others appear, God allows
each of us a choice to be unloving. Yet when those unattached parts of the
self become connected to others, our ability to tolerate loss of love from
others increases. The more we internalize, the less we need the world to
approve of us constantly. This is a hallmark of maturity. Loved people can
feel loved even when their circumstances are emotionally dry. This is the
position of being rooted and grounded in love.

JOHN TOWNSEND, *HIDING FROM LOVE*

Meditate on Scripture

The LORD himself goes before you and will be with you; he will never
leave you nor forsake you. Do not be afraid; do not be discouraged.
(Deuteronomy 31:8)

All my longings lie open before you, O Lord;
  my sighing is not hidden from you. . . .
O LORD, do not forsake me;
  be not far from me, O my God.
Come quickly to help me,
  O Lord my Savior. (Psalm 38:9, 21-22)

Those who know your name will trust in you,
  for you, O LORD, have never forsaken those who seek you.
(Psalm 9:10)

Do not hide Your face from me,
Do not turn Your servant away in anger;
You have been my help;
Do not abandon me nor forsake me,
O God of my salvation!
For my father and my mother have forsaken me,
But the LORD will take me up. (Psalm 27:9-10 NASB)

"Can a mother forget the baby at her breast
  And have no compassion on the child she has borne?
Though she may forget,
  I will not forget you!
See, I have engraved you on the palms of my hands."
(Isaiah 49:15-16)

In your midst I will leave
A humble and lowly people,
And those who are left in Israel will seek refuge in the name of Yahweh. . . .
They will be able to graze and rest
With no one to disturb them.

Shout for joy, daughter of Zion,
Israel, shout aloud!
Rejoice, exult with all your heart,
daughter of Jerusalem! . . .
Yahweh, the king of Israel, is in your midst;
You have no more evil to fear. . . .

Yahweh your God is in your midst,
A victorious warrior.
He will exult with joy over you,
He will renew you by his love;
He will dance with shouts of joy for you
As on a day of festival. (Zephaniah 3:12, 13-15, 17 JB)

Having loved His own who were in the world, He loved them to the
end. (John 13:1 NASB)

Journal Your Thoughts

Consider your own experience with abandonment. When have you felt
God's presence envelope you, safely and securely? Let your journal become
the receptacle for your thoughts, emotions, doubts, fears.

Respond in Prayer

Be still and let the words of praise come from the deepest part of your heart.
Even in dark times, remembering who God is and trusting God's character
bring us to a place of reconciliation with our own brokenness and nothing-
ness and with God's goodness. Invite the Holy Spirit to search out areas of

sin. Finally, bring your needs and fears "boldly to the throne of grace" (Hebrews 4:16 NKJV) and receive mercy and grace in time of need.

Consider Creation

Take time to stretch your limbs in God's creation. Say with the psalmist:

> I'm sure now I'll see God's goodness
> in the exuberant earth!
> Stay with GOD!
> Take heart. Don't quit.
> I'll say it again:
> Stay with GOD. (Psalm 27:13-14 *The Message*)

Seek Stillness

Move in silence toward that wound in your soul. Invite Christ into that place, to feel the pain there and to love you in your feeling of abandonment. Let him hold you in the stillness and love you. Rest, friend, safe and secure in the Shepherd's arms.

Reflection Questions

What memories or feelings does abandonment raise? When did you experience abandonment as a child? as an adult? What relationships perpetuate your abandonment feelings? What boundaries might establish safety in relationships?

How has abandonment affected your adult relationships with loved ones?

with coworkers? with people at church and in the neighborhood? In what primary ways does this fear show itself?

When have you felt abandoned by God? How did you move back into God's presence, or did the experience keep you separated?

Abandonment, anger and unforgiveness travel together. What soul business needs to be settled with God and your past before you grow in this area? What makes you feel safe in a relationship? How can you relinquish your fears and enter into your relationships more freely, with abandon?

What would change in the way you treat others, the way you share the good news of Christ with others if you no longer feared abandonment?

Hymn of Praise

"How Firm a Foundation"

Fear not, I am with thee, O be not dismayed,
For I am thy God and will still give thee aid;
I'll strengthen and help thee, and cause thee to stand
Upheld by my righteous, omnipotent hand.

When through the deep waters I call thee to go,
The rivers of woe shall not thee overflow;
For I will be with thee, thy troubles to bless,
And sanctify to thee thy deepest distress.

The soul that on Jesus has leaned for repose,
I will not, I will not desert to its foes;
That soul, though all hell should endeavor to shake,
I'll never, no never, no never forsake.

JOHN RIPPON, 1787

Examen of Conscience

As you move back through your day with Christ at your side, notice places where you felt abandoned and acted inappropriately. What about places where you took that abandonment or shame to God and hid yourself in that love? Ask God for healing, for grace and for deep release in your soul as you rest this night.

4 ⊗ THE SPOTLIGHT SELF

Seeking Balance in Solitude

"Your husband is so funny," a coworker told Robin. Another employee said, "What a sensitive man. He must be a great dad and husband." Robin watched her husband, Greg, laugh it up with colleagues at his company party. He hugged the women, slapped the men on the back, listened closely to others' stories and exuded well-being.

"Who is this man?" Robin thought. His best characteristics evidently accompanied him to work. At home, Greg reverted into glumness, snapped at the children, disciplined them harshly, then offered treats to make up with them. "He does all his living at the office."

I, on the other hand, have potluck syndrome. As a pastor's wife, many times I struggled with settings where meet 'n' greet was the order of the day. I don't do potluck talk well and am better one-on-one or leading a group into a meaty subject or else up front with a microphone.

Our public persona bears little resemblance to our private self. Loved ones don't recognize us in our "Sunday best"—when we have put on our happy face and run off to do our good deeds. Or we are relaxed and relational at home, but timid, shy, fearful or angry in public.

Should I avoid places where I am uncomfortable because it's "not my personality type"? Or should Robin's husband move out and live someplace where life is a continual party, because he is extroverted?

No. We need to return to God as our resting place, find our self-worth in

God's love and move into settings inviting the Christ in us to connect with the hungry heart of another person.

Because we focus on the milieu where we receive the most positive attention, we may live the most deeply there, feel the most alive in that place. Like a body builder with a poor workout plan, we develop only half of our spirituality, and not the supporting musculature. Part of our soul is like an emaciated muscle after weeks in a cast.

THE SPOTLIGHT SELF

Unless we live alone in a cave, we have a spotlight self, where we interact with others. Here we employ many of the gifts we are given for the kingdom; here is frequently where our talents and skills appear. Here we participate in God's work in God's way in the lives of others. Our spotlight self puts a public face on God. This is good, the way God intended.

But this performer also shows up where our reception tends to be conditional: people love us if we are profound or display amazing acumen or demonstrate superior job performance, deliver a rousing or fun speech, pray a deep prayer, volunteer heavily. We become the person who will be loved and accepted and applauded. We do not know who we are without our accolades. We lose our self in the act.

Our performance self times its entrance smoothly, waiting in the wings for the cue to appear on the stage of our life. We don't have to be professional musicians or actors or speakers to have a performance self: this spotlight self is a legitimate part of who we are. But only a part, and it is a part that is easily misread.

The public self isn't our total identity.

THE SOLITUDE SELF

Our private self is who we are when we are not looking for accolades or a date or a raise. This is who we are when we are alone, when performance doesn't matter. When we are safe. When we know we are loved no matter what.

Unfortunately, many of us don't ever know that—not in our deepest parts—and so we live more and more in places where we perform well because of love and applause. As a result the core of our being shrivels. We are like a last year's Easter egg, perfect outside but dried up and wasted on the inside. We are shadows of our potential when we ignore the interior self. But our relationship with God and others has no honest context if we do not know ourself. In solitude, in God's never-leaving loving presence, we can afford total honesty about failures and tendencies toward sin. In solitude I face my ugliness, unforgiveness, anger, laziness with others—including God. In solitude I also find, miraculously, hope—the capacity to love, forgive, grow, rest. There I notice gifts and dreams and hopes, in spite of broken places.

This balance, knowing both brokenness and progress toward wholeness, allows us to function honestly in places where the spotlight shines and we pull in a paycheck. Where we of necessity perform.

In solitude the wounds from the world begin to heal. Pain prepares us for our passion as we work it through in solitude and in accountability relationships. Here we fill up after pouring out, replenishing the well for further spotlight life and service. Just as hours of vocal disciplines practiced in private prepare the singer for the stage, so our hours of solitude, practicing God's presence, silence, praise and confession prepare us to be in the presence of others who need a life-changing encounter with the God who changes us.

INTEGRITY

One of the few things I remember about math is that an integer is a whole number. From the word *integer* we get our word *integrity*, whose root means "complete, undivided," wholeness of person. When it comes to our spotlight and our solitude selves, we find wholeness only in balance. Neither persona is complete in and of itself.

Transitioning between the two places can be rough. At home—or at the store or the gas station or on the phone with the clerk who billed us incorrectly and should know better—the mask falls off. And the more disconnected the public person from the private, the harsher the transition.

An undeveloped solitude self will atrophy our soul and catch up with our spotlight self. We will end up on stage, unable to say our lines from our heart, by heart, because our hearts are empty. Or, swallowed by hollowness, we will dash it all and vacate—our lives, our heart, our faith, our family, our job, our dreams. To neglect our solitude self is to risk slipping into sin.

Integrity requires that increasingly the two parts of our being pull closer and closer together, so that we bring more of our soul to our public persona and more of our external, public gifts to our intimate circles of loved ones. Socrates said, "May the inward and outward be at one." Then, wherever we are, we—and God's love and reputation—are in the light. We shine God's love in the spotlight of our loved ones' eyes as well.

BLINDED BY THE LIGHT

We don't live in a world requiring integrity, at least not personally. We do expect it in Christian celebrities, however, because then we can live vicariously on their persona. We substitute their success for our failures, and their failures help us avoid facing our own fallings. But how angry we are when they fall!

A Nashville pastor told *Billboard*, "We dress people up, put make-up on them, have stylists do their hair, put them on a stage in front of thousands of people, shine a spotlight on them, and then expect them to be humble." We know the stories of the legends who fell and have judged them harshly for it.

Eventually, we too will be caught in the limelight of falsity.

When Rich and I were in seminary as newlyweds, after the insanity of our lives blew away the honeymoon fog, the anxiety of those early marriage days hit me hard. I thought I was pretty cool before we got married. Only in the deep relationship of marriage did the broken glass in my soul push through. I quit performing. Too often I blew up at Rich before leaving to waitress, and en route I felt sick because of my behavior. I could not possibly smile my way into work and serve customers graciously knowing I had sandblasted my husband minutes before. God would not let me live with that breach of integrity, and as soon as possible I fed coins to the pay phone at the back of the restaurant to ask for forgiveness.

But this is not always the case with me. I have gone to church in absolute fury and pretended to be fine. I have humbly thanked people at speaking engagements and then berated the bank teller. Been sweet to an editor on the phone only to hear my child ask Rich as I hung up, "Daddy, why is Mommy so nice on the phone and not with us?"

We live double lives. And it will destroy us.

But there are problems too with focusing only on the solitude self.

INNER IMBALANCE

One woman said, "I could stay inside all day, praying and reading the Bible." The problem? With a husband and two small children, her lack of interaction with them and others dwarfed her personality. Solitude became escapism. Aloneness masked self-esteem and abandonment issues, and her circle shrank so that she rarely left home. Because they didn't get to experience Christ living and loving through her, the community was gypped.

Spiritual disciplines are intended to transform us for the sake of others. What God is doing in us, he also wants to do through us. We need community to scrape off and sand down our rough edges, to test out the truth of the gospel, to see if Jesus is real in the real world, the world outside our protective inner environs, to see if it really works, this being alone with Jesus, if he really does transform lives.

People bring us into balance and invite us into wholeness, proving whether solitude really changes us. Without relationships, who challenges our spirituality and integrity?

Once I returned from a personal retreat and found the house I'd cleaned carefully the day before wrecked. Dishes on the counter, backpacks regurgitated, toys carpeting the floor. My solitude slid away and I tumbled into taskmaster mode. What I missed was that the kids and Rich had taken hours building a special rack to hold all my pots and pans, and were proudly waiting for me to notice their handiwork, their gift of love.

The solitude didn't transform me too much. If this is what a day away with Jesus does, I'd better stay home.

REAL TRANSFORMATION

Solitude is merely isolation if it doesn't change us. It becomes an excuse to remain distant and emotionally isolated. What we do with our brain and spirit in solitude determines its effectiveness. For instance, I noticed that I spent a good deal of time either rephrasing and rehashing what I'd said into a microphone or justifying my interactions with someone else—husband, extended family, front-desk personnel. I might journal about indignities rather than invite Christ to show me where I left his side in an encounter.

Solitude can become simply aloneness if we become self-serving and isolationist, if we don't seek Christ's face, if we fail to invite him to search our hearts, heal our wounds and cleanse us of sin, and help us become whole. God's unreserved acceptance of us frees us from finding our worth in others' opinions of us, in their applause or validation. Our actions no longer need to justify us, and the spotlight becomes a place of loving others.

These two parts, solitude and public, combine to make a whole, and the more deliberate we are about integrity, the more our public and private selves will resemble one another. Public life is often full-throttle, a place where none of us is intended to dwell entirely. And if we are most alive in public, what message do we send loved ones? "I am not fully alive with you. I feel dead around you. I do all my living at work. Away from you." We all lose.

We must take responsibility for where we will be alive—both on- and off-stage. But we must also know that every plot has an antagonist.

THE ANTAGONIST

Our drama always has a crazy-maker, the one creating chaos and conflict, and this particular one "masquerades as an angel of light" (2 Corinthians 11:14). This is the deceiver, dressed for a well-rehearsed role. He will whisper that we deserve applause. He will encourage self-serving behavior. He will feed us lies for lunch and cheer when we double over from food poisoning. He will belittle our stabs at solitude, whip us with failures both personal and professional.

He will try to keep our split personality splintered, separated. He will confuse us with polish and posing when we need passion. He will nurture our egos and starve our souls. He will burn us with the limelight. He will shame us with our need for love.

Don't listen to the lies and half-truths. They are coaching cues from a fallen actor who can't wait for us to fall from grace as well. There is no shame in our longing and need for love.

THE "WATCH ME" SELF

A little boy, cute as a sprite, swims with his bright safety vest. The shallow water laps on the steps, and he paddles back and forth on the wide ledge. His dad sits in a lounge chair five feet away, focusing on his electronic palm gadget.

"Watch me! Daddy, watch me!" the child cries in his hoarse, chirping voice. The father responds every tenth time his son calls him.

Silent tears slip down my cheeks as I watch from the balcony of my room. Watch the dad *not* watch his son. Watch the son, who doesn't know I am present, perform for his dad's notice. And, as though on a split-screen TV, I watch a film clip of my own life, first as a watch-me child and then as an inattentive parent, not noticing all the watch-me moments in my children's lives because of distraction, fatigue or just plain laziness.

We all have a "watch me" side, a part of us that needs to be the complete center of attention, the focus of another's love and approval.

This is one of the roles parents play—or are intended to play—in our lives. But most of us exit childhood with a watch-me deficit, and because we are designed with that need for love and attention, we find alternate means of meeting it.

This watch-me deficit may lead us to expect a watching public to fulfill that need for love and approval; or we may focus on a miracle lover or adoring children to dote on us, filling the cavernous longing within.

That cave is best filled by the loving, attentive, smiling, forgiving, gracious presence of God. The One who knows all our blind spots and loves us anyway. The One who has watched us perform, seen us fumble the cold read, blow our lines, miss our cues, forget the blocking, upstage our colleagues, and still beams love at us. Perhaps that is the only spotlight we really need.

THE WHYS AND WHEREFORES

When I move between both worlds, it helps to ask, Why am I here? How does God want me to love others in this place? How do I make Jesus look? And to pray steadily, Help me, God. This is about you. About the people I'm with. People always knew when Moses had been with God, because his face reflected God's brilliance (Exodus 34:33-35). And if we have not been in God's presence, that too will show up on our face and in our actions. If our spotlight self is not a continuation of our solitude and private self, then the system is breached.

Our ability to love others is the measure of our Christianity and our soul. How am I loving? And what was Jesus' greatest command? "Love the LORD your God with all your heart, with all your soul, with all your mind, and with all your strength." And then, "Love your neighbor as yourself" (Mark 12:30-31). Whether our neighbor is our spouse or child or boss or the bus driver, they all hunger for a taste of heaven—through our loving.

BALANCING ACT

God also helps bring integrity between my two personas through a covenant group—five women who know my worst stories and still love me. After meeting together for a decade, they adeptly ask clarifying questions, dispelling my emotional haze. Seeing my crocodile tears—places where I sin first and grieve second—they ask, "What will be different now, Jane? What will you change about the way you live?" They pinpoint, kindly, my tendency toward isolation and unwillingness to reach out even to those closest to me, my refusal to risk relationally.

And they invite me to be whole. Holy.

Regardless of our roles, we need people who will see the spotlight self for what it is: an incomplete, partial showing of who I am; a mere portion of who God designed me to be.

We all live public lives; our relationship with Christ is constantly on display before a watching, watch-me world. We need people who are not impressed by our gifts, who maybe have never even seen those gifts in use. People who dare to challenge us to go deeper, to help us sort out lies from reality, to be discontent with anything less than a rich life with God and through God, a life that transforms the world. A life that begins by time in solitude and like yeast works its way through our being into our actions.

Friends who are committed to our wholeness likewise call us lovingly into growth. One friend and I talk deeply twice a month and e-mail in between, checking on each other's heart and soul, praying together. A spiritual director, one who listens to our lives and invites us to seek God in the Scriptures to hear how to live, can play a vital balancing part. How do we find these people? Ask, seek, knock. I started by praying for people to love me with God's love, to speak the truth from that center. Then I watched, asked questions, listened for people's soul to show up. And then I asked, "Would you consider . . . ?" James said, "You do not have, because you do not ask" (James 4:2).

Small groups break through the "we don't need relationships" myth and invite us into community, vulnerability and acceptance. They challenge us beyond "that's just the way I am" living. Families and roommates are privy to disparity between our stage and dressing room, and we can free them to ask hard questions. In solitude we sit with those questions, viewing family as part of the refining process God uses to eliminate the fool's gold from the pan of our life.

Our core belief may sound something like, "If I tell you what I really think, you won't like me. If I tell you what I'm really like, you'll leave me." To be open to the questioning of our deepest motives and longings requires putting aside our easily accessed shame reservoir. When a loved one asks, "What did that behavior mean? How does it fit with who you are called to be?" we refuse to bow to shame, which would lead to an angry reaction on our part. We listen instead to the voice of the Holy Spirit whispering through the hope and hurt of those who love us most.

And we must continue to listen deeply to our never-leaving Lover. Here is our true salvation. Here is where integrity begins, where the disintegrity, the crumbling of our wholeness, gets addressed and rectified. Where we are put back together, piece by jagged piece.

ANTIDOTE TO SOUL DISINTEGRATION

When we move to the solitude self, *we* are still the center unless we turn to God in worship. Praise is fundamental to integrity, shifting the focus from *us* and beaming it on God. Praise moves us toward humility, acknowledging God's lordship in our lives and our world. Any good that ever conceivably comes as a result of our using our gifts and graces in this world comes because of God's amazing ability to bring gold out of dross, to use foolish things to bring him glory. Everything that we have and do and are and accomplish is because of God's immense love for us and empowerment of us. To ever believe otherwise is a step toward breakdown.

Sometimes, after I lead a retreat or speak at a convention, I head toward the car or airplane and start to call my prayer partners, to "report in" about the time, how God showed up.

I have to stop myself from reaching for my cell phone; I must turn instead to God. To move wholly into that accepting, glowing presence where the spotlight of love never dims or burns out. To focus on God's amazing work, the grace that allows me to participate in the kingdom even with all my flaws and move humbly into praise and thanksgiving and deep gratitude.

When we walk off the stage of our lives—lock our office door, turn off the computer, shut the sales ledger, flip the "Closed" sign on the door, put away our cleaning supplies, turn in our apron, shoo the last child home—we face the most important choice of our day.

To walk into the wings and into the arms of our Shepherd, letting him lead us to places that will restore our soul. May he restore your soul, in this time today.

FOR YOUR RETREAT

Quotes to Contemplate

The Paris Opera House . . . sits on three acres of land, and four-fifths of the theater is backstage. . . . The backstage design ensured the onstage success.

DOUGLAS RUMFORD, *SOULSHAPING*

Silent solitude forges true speech.

BRENNAN MANNING, *ABBA'S CHILD*

A character gap develops when we allow activity in the outer world to distract us from the daily business of bringing our attitudes, desires, words, and behavior under the sanctifying power of the Holy Spirit. Character is like physical exercise or any form of learning; you cannot "cram," hoping to do in a day or week what can only be accomplished by months and years of consistent practice.

DOUGLAS RUMFORD, *SOULSHAPING*

A persuaded mind and even a well-intentioned heart is a long way from exact and faithful practice. Nothing has been more common in every age, and still more so today, than meeting souls who are perfect and saintly in speculation. . . . True spirituality is not leisure-time activity, a diversion from life. It is essentially subversive, and the test of its genuineness is practical.

FRANÇOIS FÉNELON, C. 1651-1715, *CHRISTIAN PERFECTION*

All actual life is encounter.

MARTIN BUBER, *I AND THOU*

Out of his solitude Jesus reached out his caring hand to the people in need. In the lonely place his care grew strong and mature. And from there he entered into a healing closeness with his fellow human beings.

To care means first of all to be present to each other. From experience, you know that those who care for you become present to you. When they listen, they listen to you. When they speak, you know they speak to you. And when they ask questions, you know it is for your sake and not for their own. Their presence is a healing presence because they accept you on your terms, and they encourage you to take your own life seriously and to trust your own vocation.

HENRI J. M. NOUWEN, *OUT OF SOLITUDE*

It is not physical solitude that actually separates one from other(s), not physical isolation, but spiritual isolation. . . . When one is a stranger to oneself then one is estranged from others too. If one is out of touch with oneself, then one cannot touch others.

ANNE MORROW LINDBERG, *GIFT FROM THE SEA*

Meditate on Scripture

God is light; in him there is no darkness at all. If we claim to have fellowship with him yet walk in the darkness, we lie and do not live by the truth. But if we walk in the light, as he is in the light, we have fellowship with one another, and the blood of Jesus, his Son, purifies us from all sin. (1 John 1:5-7)

If I speak in the tongues of men and of angels, but have not love, I am only a resounding gong or a clanging cymbal. If I have the gift of prophecy and can fathom all mysteries and all knowledge, and if I have a faith that can move mountains, but have not love, I am nothing. If I give all I possess to the poor and surrender my body to the flames, but have not love, I gain nothing. (1 Corinthians 13:1-3)

To him who is able to keep you from falling and to present you before his glorious presence without fault and with great joy—to the only God our Savior be glory, majesty, power and authority, through Jesus Christ our Lord, before all ages, now and forevermore! Amen. (Jude 24-25)

Your adornment must not be merely external; . . . but let it be the hidden person of the heart, with the imperishable quality of a gentle and quiet spirit, which is precious in the sight of God. (1 Peter 3:3-4 NASB)

Therefore, since through God's mercy we have this ministry, we do not lose heart. Rather, we have renounced secret and shameful ways; we do not use deception, nor do we distort the word of God. On the contrary, by setting forth the truth plainly we commend ourselves to every man's conscience in the sight of God. . . .

So we make it our goal to please him, whether we are at home in the body or away from it. For we all must appear before the judgment seat of Christ, that each one may receive what is due him for the things done while in the body, whether good or bad. (2 Corinthians 4:1-2; 5:9, 10)

Anyone who claims to be in the light but hates his brother is still in the darkness. Whoever loves his brother lives in the light, and there is nothing in him to make him stumble. (1 John 2:9-10)

Journal Your Thoughts

Reflect on your spotlight and solitude selves. Where is there disparity? Integrity? Journal before God about your longings in both places. Where have you damaged others by living and functioning out of only part of your being?

Respond in Prayer

Focus on your heart, on the places where pain ruptures, failure shames, people are wounded. What a gift to release poor performances and emaciated souls to God, find freedom in confession and forgiveness, and to look at God. Praise shifts our heart from our faults to God's fullness.

Consider Creation

As you participate in God's creation, where do you see examples of balance between the public and private in nature? The rhythm of day and night, sunlight and dark earth, root growth and above-ground flourishing. Let God feed your heart in these places of beauty and fortify you for reentry to the fray of life.

Seek Stillness

The psalmist reminds us:

I have stilled and quieted my soul;
    like a weaned child with its mother,
    like a weaned child is my soul within me.

O Israel, put your hope in the LORD
   both now and forevermore. (Psalm 131:2-3)

In stillness let your heart settle, the disparity of spotlight and solitude dissolve. Invite the Holy Spirit to open you to God's presence.

Reflection Questions

Where do you feel most alive? In what arenas do you find yourself performing, using a false mask to cover your inner self? Identify some of your spotlight behaviors.

When do you sense a brokenness between who you are in public and who you are with people you love? Does this occur when you are in solitude with God?

How do you nurture your solitude self? When have you found yourself without enough inner fuel to power your public self? What happened there?

What accountability do you have for integrity? Who asks you the hard questions, invites you into wholeness? When is it hardest to listen, and with whom? What happens within you and how do you respond? How will you find accountability people?

What would it look like for the Shepherd to restore your soul? What would have to change about the way you are living? What is your greatest longing?

Hymn of Praise

"Jesu, Thy Boundless Love to Me"

Jesu, thy boundless love to me
   no thought can reach, no tongue declare;

O knit my thankful heart to thee,
and reign without a rival there.
Thine wholly, thine alone, I am;
be thou alone my constant flame.
O Love, how cheering is thy ray!
All pain before thy presence flies,
Care, anguish, sorrow, melt away,
where'er thy healing beams arise;
O Jesu, nothing may I see,
Nothing desire, or seek, but thee!

PAUL GERHARDT, 1653; TRANS. JOHN WESLEY, 1739

Examen of Conscience

As evening closes, replay your day with God. When was there deep interaction with Christ? Where did you withdraw from him, moving into performance mode? Where was there integrity between spotlight and solitude? Where did God meet your need to be the focus of loving attention and affirmation? Move back through your day and beckon God's healing presence.

5 ⚏ DEPRESSION AND FAITH

Finding Your Way Back to the Light

I can't hit the high notes anymore—I've lost the upper register of my emotions and can feel only the deep, haunting, sorrowful notes of the bass clef. Cried this morning as I contemplated antidepressants, and wonder if I have always been depressed. When didn't I feel this pulling sadness on my soul? Yesterday disappeared in anger and hurt and feelings of abandonment. I again gave up power so I could nurse my wounded soul.

I am regressing, slipping away. It scares me. I'm so tired of fighting this darkness. I am tired of existing without any feeling. My family has been short-changed by my depressed living. Something has to change, Father. I don't want to live with the loss of feeling or with just the shadows. My self-loathing is huge right now. Oh God, please help me. I do not have the energy to help myself.

I have not uttered the D-word regarding my own state of mind and soul in six years; I have watched the darkness come and kept moving to avoid it. But this day, this week, this month, I did not fight. I did not run. I caved in on myself and sank into the pool of darkness. It is hard to find comfort in God, to experience the Shepherd as a resting place in the valley of depression.

I am not alone in the dark. Twenty-five percent of us will at some time experience a biochemical change in the brain that may be diagnosed as mental illness. The number of people who suffer from a serious depressive episode in any given year is roughly ten million, yet because of the social and spiritual stigma associated with this misunderstood malady, the church may not know how to respond. If you or someone you love is affected by depression, there is hope, there are means of coping.

DESCRIBING THE DARKNESS

Depression is a silent, insidious illness of body and soul that manifests itself in the mind. This chapter's opening quote, excerpted from my journal, illustrates a time when I touched its dark shores.[1] I have lived in that darkness for varying lengths of time, with various means of escape, some legitimate, some simply other means of avoiding my pain.

Depression can take many forms, from the blues, seasonal affective disorder (SAD) and postpartum depression, to the biochemically based bipolar (manic) and unipolar (clinical) depression. This broad spectrum can make depression difficult to diagnose, and fewer than half the people suffering from depression will seek any medical treatment at all, preferring to suffer in silence rather than risk the stigma of being diagnosed with a mental illness.

Unfortunately, many people still do not consider depression a legitimate illness.

Symptoms vary. Nancy couldn't stop crying. Jerry, loved for his humor and energy at his business, couldn't drag himself from bed. Jan's depression-related panic attacks resulted in agoraphobia. Sandy quit her job because of lowered productivity and difficulty with stress. Ed went to work later and later, and his attitude toward coworkers displayed anger and edginess. Larry blamed his family and left home. Joann's artwork grew darker, bleaker. By nature serious, Russell became the church jokester and started charging massive amounts on credit cards.

Other common symptoms include feeling sad, hopeless or worthless; trouble sleeping or sleeping too much; difficulty concentrating and forget-

---

[1]This chapter is a layperson's experience, a collection of reference and research and real-life stories that might enlighten the person who struggles in the occasional darkness of depression, and point them toward the light. It is not meant to be a psychiatric look at a potentially serious problem. The suggestions of this chapter are not intended to substitute for counseling or consultation with your physician.

fulness; unexplained low energy or fatigue; anxiety; loss of interest or pleasure; and changes in weight or appetite.

A COSTLY ILLNESS

Depression robs its victims of joy and simple pleasure, of laughter and feelings. It wreaks havoc on our work and relationships, draining our families of vitality, depriving others of our gifts of attention, service and love. Pulling the cloak of depression tightly, I withdrew, wielding it like a club to keep people away. Isolation can contribute to the downward spiral.

Income loss due to depression is a concern. When Ted lost his job, he plunged into depression, and his wife, who needed to keep her job, could not leave him alone. Her employer is holding her position temporarily, but she is without pay. Still, the widely held myths in church and society keep many in the dark about depression and ratchet up the cost to all involved.

MYTHS ABOUT DEPRESSION

Christians shouldn't get angry or depressed. Depression is neither a character flaw nor a sign of weak faith or spiritual immaturity. Like cancer or diabetes, endogenous depression is a physical problem, such as chemical imbalance, with mental symptoms. Externally caused (exogenous) depression results from agents outside of ourselves, such as grief, stress or pain.

Is this unscriptural? Look at how King David managed his emotional life: he either leaped around praising God, called down invectives on the enemy or begged God to lift his head, to restore the joy of his salvation (see 2 Samuel 6:14-16; Psalm 3:3-4; 51; 139:19-22). He pulsated with a full spectrum of feelings. The difference between David and many Christians is that he recognized and voiced his depression. The king invited God into the process of restoration, confident that with the Lord's help the depression could deepen his faith and bring him back into a sense of God's presence.

Elijah's enormous spiritual and physical workout with the false priests depleted him. Depression often sweeps in after moments of significant spiritual accomplishment, as Elijah experienced after slaying the false prophets (see 1 Kings 18—19:5). We can blame the enemy—and Satan certainly is capable of taking advantage of us at such a time—but research shows a correlation between stressful (albeit victorious) situations and resultant slumps of energy and adrenaline, all of which increase the likelihood of depression.

Snap out of it! Allison's sister didn't understand Allison's depression after a messy and lengthy divorce and the fallout of helping her children cope with the changes and traumas as a single mother. Her sister's advice: Get over it.

Mild depression is a normal response to life and loss. Failure to respect this grief cycle can short-circuit the healthy process of working through pain and loss, leading the afflicted into denial and a steeper downward spiral. When we honor people's time in dealing with depression, we foster empathy and support, and actually encourage the depressive to continue to journey through the shadows into the light.

Depression is a pity party. Stop focusing on yourself, and you'll be fine. Jerry moved his family thousands of miles, exchanging a lifelong dream for financial solvency. He unpacked, made necessary repairs, assisted with the running of the house and went to his new job. His wife blew up when he couldn't haul himself to church and didn't want to participate in social functions. "It's a pity party," she said. "He's being selfish and ignoring his family's needs."

Sometimes depression results from focusing on others to the exclusion of our own healthy and normal needs. Depression can be a healing process if we allow ourselves time to examine its roots and learn about ourselves, our needs and dreams, as well as our failures and shortcomings. This can, of course, become a pity party if we refuse to consider appropriate tools given for recovery from depression.

These responses all overlook the fact that depression is an illness. Underlying issues can offer clarity.

UNDERLYING ISSUES

False guilt and self-blame can immobilize the depressive. Rooting out the hidden issues contributing to depression involves careful digging in the soil of our hearts. Read through and reflect on this list before God, asking him to show you where you or a loved one need help.

Stress and trauma. Stress is a key factor in psychologically induced depression, especially stress due to trauma or loss. People with physical or sexual abuse in their past or present are also susceptible, as are those suffering from chronic pain or a serious or protracted illness. Cancer treatment, certain steroids and other medications may lead to depression. Consult your physician and bring a list of medications to be certain.

Past pain and grief. Depression is a warning frozen in icy darkness: Unresolved pain fossilized here. Depression often veils us from our pain, from the grief necessary to recover from loss or change in our lives. For instance, people who had a loved one die when they were young are at least twice as likely to suffer from major depression as those who have not experienced a similar loss. Grief is a natural and necessary means of moving out of depression.

Fear. Fear can contribute to depression. Fear of what others think of us, of authority figures, of failure, of imperfection, of physical danger: all these keep us self-contained, closed up and isolated.

Shame. Lewis Smedes writes, "I lugged around inside me a dead weight of not-good-enoughness." Unrecognized, shame can plummet us into depression. Some of shame's symptoms:

- Shame includes an enduring negative self-image.
- Shame is highly "performance conscious."
- Shame makes you unaware of personal boundaries.
- Shames festers in people who are "wounded."
- Shame is accompanied by a pervading tiredness.
- Shame has a built-in radar system, tuned to keeping everyone happy and at peace.
- Shame makes you ignore your own needs like a martyr.
- Shame tends toward addictive behavior, which can manifest itself in overinvolvement in work or ministry.

- Shame has no concept of "normal."
- Shame makes it difficult to trust others.
- Shame makes you possessive in relationships.
- Shame has a high need for control.

Unforgiveness. Hauling unforgiveness around is like swimming with iron skillets for flippers. We know we're supposed to forgive, but sometimes pride or pain over being hurt prevents us from releasing both ourself and the unforgiven person of the burden. Ignored, unforgiveness can sink us into the waters of depression.

Loss of self. The more distanced we become from the person God created us to be, the more likely we are to become depressed. Years ago, when finally naming the pervasive darkness, I realized I had never understood the nameless yearning of my soul. Disguising—and avoiding—myself by excessively meeting others' needs, I lost myself. Depression was my soul's attempt to gain my attention and bring me to healing.

Anger. When talking about depression, a friend said, "If I am depressed, I need for you to ask me what I am angry about." Anger creates a vortex pulling us into depression: anger at ourselves, at others, at God. But because we worry, taught that anger isn't spiritual, we bury it. As it tunnels into a soul, depression results.

Notice the interconnection between fear, rage, depression and lack of control. Tracy Thompson writes:

> By this time, depression had taken over my brain, and sleep was its first casualty. I was an insomniac, irritable, raging at the slightest noise in the night, a caldron of anger during the day. After years of suppressing rage, I now felt like a volcano in continuous eruption. Any minor inconvenience could set me off—misplacing a blouse, getting lost somewhere, . . . finding myself stalled in a traffic jam. I felt I was going out of control. My fear of doing so was at war with my overwhelming need to express this constant, nameless fury in some physical way. I threw things; I beat helplessly on the floor.

SPIRITUAL ATTACK

We would be foolish not to mention how much the enemy loves to mess with our mind. Satan will pull us down any way possible. This may look like dizziness, dark thoughts, suicidal impulses. In 1527, Martin Luther experienced such severe dizziness he had to stop preaching and leave the pulpit. After years of intense reformation work, he suffered ruthless depression. Months later an intense buzzing in his ear forced him to lie down. "He became cold, and he was convinced he had seen his last night. In a loud prayer, he surrendered himself to God's will."

With medical help, Luther regained partial strength. But depression and illness overcame him repeatedly that year. Of one of his bouts, he wrote a friend, "I spent more than a week in death and hell. My entire body was in pain, and I still tremble. Completely abandoned by Christ, I labored under the vacillations and storms of desperation and blasphemy against God. But through the prayers of the saints [his friends], God began to have mercy on me and pulled my soul from the inferno below."

How do we know if depression is enemy-induced? If traditional means of combating depression do not work or no reasons for the depression seem apparent, such as a chemical imbalance or exogenous factors, don't underestimate the power of the enemy. I consider current ministry endeavors and relationship issues. When we are engaged in strategic battles, Satan can be expected on the scene disguised as all sorts of physical maladies. Prior to certain speaking engagements, I have experienced dizziness so severe that I could not move my eyes without extreme nausea. Nothing stopped the dizziness but the name of Jesus. Enemy warfare can only be fought in Christ's power, and sometimes it takes repeated rebuking of the enemy. Whether Satan is involved or not, shaking free from the underlying causes of depression is a spiritual battle.

COPING WITH DEPRESSION

Learning about ourself is a principle tool for recovery. When do we become depressed? For Ginger, depression strikes when she is overwhelmed with heavy responsibilities, busyness and lack of sleep. Mark's clinical depression became apparent after several years in the wrong job. After beginning to listen to his true calling, he was able to leave the antidepressants behind.

Talia struggled through months of depression and emerged stronger, with a bright smile and an empathic spirit. "I had to develop a toolbox to rebuild my life. What have I been eating? What about sleep? Exercise? Caffeine? Sugar? How much water am I drinking?"

But good self-care requires energy, a primary missing ingredient in the depressive. "I don't want to talk to my doctor," I wailed to Rich. "She will say, 'Let's look at your anger, Jane. And let's talk about your health plan.' I don't have the energy to take care of myself."

Proper nutrition and exercise become vital tools in our toolbox. A Duke University psychologist prescribed an exercise regimen for depressed patients. In four months, 60 percent of them got better—the same as those on antidepressants. Within ten months, 30 percent of the medicated patients relapsed, but only 9 percent of the exercisers.

Consulting a physician to eliminate possible biological or neurological causes is important. A safety net of strategic friends, a support group and counseling aid to recovery are also critical. Medication may be necessary because it allows the brain buzz to subside and creates pathways for logical thought and resultant action. Therapy and half an antidepressant worked for Julia.

God does not want us to live with a flat-line of the soul. Beginning to embrace our gifts and dreams activates our heart. Beauty nurtures me, and time alone with God in nature fosters some basic healing. If laughter helps, then we seek out funny people. Beginning to be honest with our loved ones is critical, because masking our depression or its contributing feelings keeps us separated and perpetuates the darkness.

Small steps toward the light can slow or reverse the downward spiral. "What one thing will you do for yourself today?" my mother-in-law asked me one day in my darkness. Luther clung to God, penning his most famous hymn in depression's pit: "A Mighty Fortress Is Our God."

Though our beds swim with tears in the night, dawn always comes. God has set a faithful witness in the sky, testifying to his steady care for us. God promises joy in the morning.

HEALING LIGHT

My throat aches from swallowing tears. My jaws clench tightly to keep the pain in. I force myself to reach out to Rich, to hold and be held, to bridge the gap between dark and light, to share the dark and no longer alienate him. With my face against his neck, a tear escapes, streaking us both with its silent despair. His strong, quiet support wraps around me, embracing me in the dark, an unwavering candle of faith and strength.

I have clutched the darkness, wallowed in it like a harlot; loved the darkness more than the light. But the night, which recedes and then sweeps back in to cover my head, I now push away, awaiting the brightness of the Christ, who said, "I am the Light of the world."

Once, when we were hiking in the Ozarks, a file of girls trickled past, exclaiming over plate-sized leaves and tiny acorns and lush spring growth. At the end of the file an older woman held the elbow of a slender reed of a girl. The blind child walked cautiously, listening as her guide helped her not only to walk but to see.

Darkness has blinded me, but like the blind men by the roadside, my soul calls, "Lord, I want you to restore my sight" (see Matthew 20:29-34).

One small step at a time, bones wobbly from passivity, I begin to move. Slowly. I drink more water. Gradually I add exercise. Eliminate some sugar and caffeine. I begin to journal and talk about my feelings, invite others into this experience with me. And I start to pray and praise. A melody will not leave my mind, and warbly sounds work their way out around the sobs.

My hope is built on nothing less
Than Jesus' blood and righteousness.
I dare not trust the sweetest frame,
But wholly trust in Jesus' Name. . . .

When darkness veils His lovely face,
I rest on His unchanging grace.
In ev'ry high and stormy gale,
My anchor holds within the veil.

His oath, His covenant, His blood,
Support me in the whelming flood.
When all around my soul gives way,
He then is all my Hope and Stay.

Just as God created the night, God created the potential for these dark, shadow times of the soul. But God also created the light to limit the night. We can barely pray in the sweeping darkness, "Lord, take the dimness of my soul away." But it is enough.

Even though I have walked through the valley of shadows, I am not alone. And like the blind girl hiking in the Ozarks, the Shepherd gently touches my elbow, leading me, guiding me, into restoration.

As you prayerfully enter this retreat time, may you know the comfort of God's rod and staff. May the Shepherd be your resting place and your light, carrying you through the dark.

FOR YOUR RETREAT

Quotes to Contemplate

Hate, anger, resentment and bitterness are chains that bind us to the past. Even if the person who hurt us dies, we usually feel trapped with the lingering pain. . . . The chains of memories of painful hurts become twisted with self-serving inaccuracies over time. We may try to toss off the chains by forgetting, but forgetting won't loose those chains. Only forgiveness will.

EVERETT L. WORTHINGTON JR., *TO FORGIVE IS HUMAN*

When depression is stigmatized as illness and weakness, a double bind is created: If we admit to depression, we will be stigmatized by others; if we feel it but do not admit it, we stigmatize ourselves, internalizing the social judgment. . . . The only remaining choice may be truly sick behavior: to experience no emotion at all.

LESLEY HAZELTON, *THE RIGHT TO FEEL BAD*

Perfectionists have the highest rate of depression among all human beings.

JOHN POWELL, *HAPPINESS IS AN INSIDE JOB*

Mental illness taught me that I can get really ill relying on myself.

Acknowledging God as a power higher than myself was all-important in my recovery. There's no doubt that God had a hand in the medication and the psychotherapy that helped me recover. But beyond such treatment, I have come to realize that prayer is where all healing begins—healing of the mind, the body, the spirit or the heart.

A PSYCHIATRIST WHO WISHES TO REMAIN ANONYMOUS

*I tore down the dark and dismal drapes
that hung like dead men on the gallows.
I threw open the windows
and cried out as the sunlight spilled into this
silent room
as surprised as I.
And as my eyes became accustomed
to this fierce and searching light,
I realized it was time to laugh again.*

SHEILA WALSH, HONESTLY

Meditate on Scripture

He reached down from on high and took hold of me;
    he drew me out of deep waters.
He rescued me from my powerful enemy,
    from my foes, who were too strong for me.
They confronted me in the day of my disaster,
    but the LORD was my support.
He brought me out into a spacious place;
    he rescued me because he delighted in me. . . .

You, O LORD, keep my lamp burning;
  my God turns my darkness into light. (Psalm 18:16-18, 28)

In the beginning was the Word, and the Word was with God, and the
Word was God. He was in the beginning with God; all things were
made through him, and without him was not anything made that was
made. In him was life, and the life was the light of men. The light
shines in the darkness, and the darkness has not overcome it. (John
1:1-5 RSV)

The people who sat in darkness
  have seen a great light,
and for those who sat in the region and shadow of death
  light has dawned. (Matthew 4:16 RSV)

But as for me, I keep watch in hope for the LORD,
  I wait for God my Savior;
  my God will hear me.
Do not gloat over me, my enemy!
  Though I have fallen, I will rise.
Though I sit in darkness,
  the LORD will be my light. (Micah 7:7-8)

For God, who said, "Let light shine out of darkness," made his light
shine in our hearts to give us the light of the knowledge of the glory
of God in the face of Christ.

  But we have this treasure in jars of clay to show that this all-surpassing
power is from God and not from us. We are hard pressed on every
side, but not crushed; perplexed, but not in despair; persecuted, but
not abandoned; struck down, but not destroyed. We always carry
around in our body the death of Jesus, so that the life of Jesus may also
be revealed in our body. (2 Corinthians 4:6-10)

Journal Your Thoughts

Journaling is a life-saving technique and helps bring clarity to the confusion of depression. It acts as a safety valve, a place to dump the darkness and find light and grace. Illuminated by God's Word, take time to note your journey and experience with depression. Notice feelings, interactions and symptoms that might lend understanding.

Respond in Prayer

Shutting God out of our dark is a natural reaction. We forget that "Even the darkness is not dark to You, / And the night is as bright as the day. / Darkness and light are alike" to God (Psalm 139:12 NASB). God is not frightened by our darkness, and inviting God's presence brings life. Don't worry about a formula prayer; just pour out your soul.

Consider Creation

As you observe creation, reflect on the interplay of dark and light, of sun and shadows. Let God speak to you of the value of both, and illumine your soul through creation.

Seek Stillness

"My soul finds rest in God alone; / my salvation comes from him" (Psalm 62:1). Rest, now, in the Shepherd's loving care and presence. Let God give you deep breaths and speak to your longing heart.

Reflection Questions

Consider these questions in light of either your own depression or your loved ones':

What experiences have you had with depression? What preconceived notions do you have about it? How has it affected you? Your family? Friends? If you struggle with depression, what are some beginning signs?

How has depression affected your self-esteem?

What support do you have in depression? Who have you brought into your circle? How do you want people to support you in the darkness?

What memories or incidents might be related to your depression? Anger, shame, past pain, unforgiveness? If there is depression in your family tree, how were you affected by that?

What is the Holy Spirit nudging you to do regarding depression?

Hymn of Praise

"A Mighty Fortress Is Our God"

A mighty fortress is our God,
A bulwark never failing;
Our helper He amid the flood
Of mortal ills prevailing;
For still our ancient foe
Doth seek to work us woe;
His craft and power are great,
And armed with cruel hate,
On earth is not his equal.

And though this world with devils filled,
Should threaten to undo us,
We will not fear, for God hath willed
His truth to triumph through us;
The Prince of Darkness grim,
We tremble not for him;
His rage we can endure,
For lo, his doom is sure;
One little word shall fell him.

That word above all earthly powers,
No thanks to them, abideth.
The spirit and the gifts are ours
Through Him who with us sideth.
Let goods and kindred go,
This mortal life also;
The body they may kill;
God's truth abideth still;
His kingdom is forever.

MARTIN LUTHER, 1529; TRANS. FREDERIC H. HEDGE, 1853

Examen of Conscience

Ask God to grip your hand and go with you through the past day. Is there darkness there? Ask for light. Is there separation? Ask God to help you move back together. Is there pain or shame? God is greater. Find grace as you turn to God in rest.

6 ⊗ IN THE MAKER'S MARK

Embracing Creativity and Spirituality

Women sat expectantly at the tables, waiting for their ice-breaker question. I heard it and groaned. "Talk about where you are creative." When my turn came, I said, "I don't consider myself creative."

A harried season in our lives had left me numb, and for months I'd been living like the Israelites, "They have forgotten their restingplace" (Jeremiah 50:6 KJV). For too long, time with the Shepherd had been limited to a speed-reading session of Scripture and a hurried prayer. Extended times with God deepen the well and allow fresh water to flow. When desperation forced me into God's arms for rest and healing, when I became serious about finding God as my resting place, my longing to live well and richly, to see God transform my past pain into passion emerged.

God can take a trashed past and create a whole new future. He is the genius recycler, never wasting our experiences but using them to help others. God is always at work, redeeming the worst and bringing forth the best.

Part of our problem is our understanding of creativity. Maxine Hancock suggests that creativity is "finding new ways of putting existing components together to make a whole." If it gives life, it is creative. My friends were actors, painters, musicians, stage managers, composers, advertising experts, lawyers. I did not share their creative gifts—my stick figures cast doubt on research suggesting an equal distribution of creative gifts. I don't paint, write music or sing, haven't a thought in my head about inventing light bulbs, and jingles are definitely not my forte.

But creativity is not limited to the flamboyant, obvious pursuits: painting, composing, sculpting. If these are not your gifts, read on. None of us stood behind the door when God doled out creativity. So you don't whittle wood or whistle arias? That creativity goes beyond the high-profile artistic forms— or even the dexterous use of duct tape—is good news.

At one time Christians were the forerunners in every area of media and market—when high ideals gave impetus to the highest, most creative quality of product. They did not try to identify their work as "Christian," but because of their personal relationship with the Creator of the universe, their commitment to excellence in expression, ethics and workmanship propelled Christians to the front. Today, we're too busy trying to keep our churches running single-handedly, too serious with the somber pursuit of holiness and godliness and pleasing everyone we know that we are exhausted at home and at work. Getting through is my goal many days. Excellence is far from our minds, much less creative excellence in our endeavors.

We shove creativity to the margins, deeming it frivolous or effeminate, losing our creative edge in the world by relegating creativity to the arena of unnecessary and irrelevant.

Yet talking with people all over the country, encouraging them to listen to their hearts and longings again, I hear a frustrated refrain. They are too tired, too beaten down in the go-fast-and-crash lane, too strapped with all the demands on them. They are depressed. They want out.

And too many do get out—by leaving their faith, abandoning their marriage, dreams, family or job; by using substances or pornography to dull the ache and help them forget. Or they use up their creativity by tubing out in front of their latest big screen TV or something else to fill the heart gap, created by the disconnect between creative yearnings and how they are living.

Don't check out yet. Instead, check this out—

SAVING GRACE

The good news is that we are all creative, every last one of us. We each bear the creative imprint of God's DNA, who said when we were created, "Yee-haw! This is amazing, outstanding, the pinnacle of my handiwork! Yes, yes, yes! High fives all around!" Others translate God's words as, "It was very good" (Genesis 1:31).

God made something out of nothing—the ultimate form of creativity—bringing into existence the entire universe. And then God made us. We are designed to live creatively, regardless of our day job and living situation and income flow and any repressed fear of super glue. We are made in God's image, according to the Scriptures, and who can argue about God's creative genius? Creativity is a base component in our makeup, inherent in our very being.

Psychological tests seem to confirm this. Alex Osborn writes, "An analysis of almost all the psychological tests ever made points to the conclusion that creative talent is normally distributed—that *all* of us possess this talent."

So: creativity is a matter of fact, not of feeling creative. We are all artists of sorts—artisans attempting to interpret life through our words, actions, life work: expressions or representations of God in the eyes of the world. We are called to be icons, signs pointing the way to the Creator. And by calling out the utmost creativity in ourselves and the body of Christ, we bring glory to God and lead others to him. The question is not *Am I creative?* but rather *How do we tap into this God-given trait?* By understanding the wild and wide variety of ways creativity appears.

TYPES OF CREATIVITY

Whether we are creative with words or widgets, a battle plan or a floor plan, we were made for creative living. And thanks be to God creativity goes beyond arts and crafts and fun with sequins. (If these are your form of creativity, I bow to you. Thank you for using your gifts. Please keep developing them so I do not have to thread sequins onto a string.)

Creativity looks like an amazing hockey power play. Or wiring the car together to keep it running until you can afford the right parts. Creativity is keeping a budget; juggling relationships and needs; balancing hearth, home and workplace; putting hundreds of meals on the table each year. Resourcefulness, ingenuity and inventiveness show up daily.

Creativity is evident in actions, hospitality, atmosphere. Creativity can transform the mundane. John Updike wrote, "Any activity becomes creative when the doer cares about doing it right, or better." Creativity shows up in relationships too. When Jim proposed to Cinda on Christmas, he wrapped her gifts in separate boxes, composed poetry for each gift, arranged them on the (frozen) lake in front of her home and invited her out to open presents. Each gift led to the next one, ending with the tiny box containing an engagement ring.

So poetry isn't your thing? You hardly have the energy to read a bedtime story to the kids or the dog? Forget worrying about rhyming words and stanzas and couplets (whatever they are). One night I dragged home with sleepy children who still needed a bedtime routine. I didn't feel like being a pitchfork from behind. "OK, kids—"

Ruthie interrupted me. "I know, brush our teeth and get our jammies on."

By God's grace, I smiled. "Nope, I was going to suggest that you both turn somersaults all the way down the hall to your room and have a race."

Maybe not the best way to wind kids down for bed, but it sure beat the exhausting monotony of routine. They went to bed smiling. And so did I.

Creativity shows up in a pinch. Too often I remember at the last minute that I need to prepare a meal and have no raw ingredients for the process. I run to the kitchen singing the Rubietta rendition of the Mother Goose rhyme:

> I went to the cupboard,
> the cupboard was bare!
> What to prepare—
> there's no food anywhere!

Minutes later, like Merlin the magician I emerge with an unlikely concoction and place a panic meal on the table. Sometimes it is all the same color or requires a vitamin or some cardboard fiber to make a complete meal. I'm rarely able to duplicate it and probably won't publish a cookbook next, but this seat-of-the-pants creation satisfies me. Plus I don't have the headaches of menu planning. Which could be someone else's exercise of creativity. What about words? You don't have to be a professional writer to use words to build others up. Mother Teresa said, "We are all pencils in the hand of God." And God needs all our pencils to write life, love and laughter in the void in people's lives. Marge's ministry is writing letters, and God has encouraged countless people through her gift.

Rich can discuss hard issues with others and never lose his temper, keeping his voice calm and kind. His example reminds me to check the ratio of negative and positive comments, and creates a desire to build up others by encouraging their good qualities. Relationships wither under harshness but blossom with tender words. That's creativity.

THE UNLIMITED GIFT OF LIMITS

A creative response to life may mean turning pain into a positive, finding a way out of a constricting situation or turning a predicament into praise or a problem into a possibility. Rollo May writes that creativity "arises out of the struggle of human beings with and against that which limits them." If, as Karen Mains says, creativity is "the ability to get away from the main track, break out of the mold, or diverge from the rest of society," then creativity is a primary trait of the walk by faith, of a people who refused to let the world squeeze them into its mold (Romans 12:2) and who wandered "in deserts and mountains, and in caves and holes in the ground" (Hebrews 11:38). Creativity means taking risks, allowing God to surge forward through the opening.

Too old to play the piano? Or paint? Maybe not. Art museums, concert halls and the patent office pulse with the works and names of people who refused to let limitations constrain them. After an abused childhood, Beethoven at age forty-six was completely deaf. He went on to write some of his greatest compositions, including five symphonies.

Though nearly blind from cataracts, Monet painted until death knocked on the door. A blind Milton penned *Paradise Lost*. Rescued from her dark, silent world by a loving teacher, Helen Keller lived her life giving hope to not only the blind and deaf but to the rest of the world as well. These people refused to be limited by life's limitations.

So much of creativity is choosing to look for—and celebrate—life in the midst of what feels like death. Attitude converts limitations into actions and creativity. When we are most limited, God is most free.

So you got bad news? The project was turned down, or you missed the promotion, or your car's engine blew up? Fix a celebration meal, acknowledge your disappointment and choose to view your status as a vital next step in God's great adventure for your life.

Our self-imposed limitations limit creativity more than circumstances. In fact, the deeper our need, the more desperate we are, the more creative we tend to be. If the mother of invention is necessity, then poverty is a real boost to creative genius. Adversity sharpens our creative edge. Don't waste any more time lamenting pain from the past. Instead, use it for good.

Did you grow up with "You can't do that" or "You can do anything you want!"? Did you hear, "Great job" or a shaming "Good grief, what are you thinking"? Were your parents enthusiastic in their embrace of life, of new ideas, of spontaneity? How we were raised may make a difference in how developed our creativity is at this point, but not in the amount of creativity we have. So get to work. Start playing. There's still time.

Grieve the wounds of those who were emotionally, physically or creatively absent. Then use those wounds to drill into your vein of passion, passion that allows you to live creatively, to make a difference in a world starved for visible expressions of the invisible God.

BENEFITS OF CREATIVITY

Creativity gives God glory, and expressing ourselves creatively reaps personal benefits as well. A creative "workout" lowers stress, builds self-confidence and increases life enjoyment. It may also affect immune function, improve health and lengthen our life. Remember your pride at bringing a special project home from school? Many groups, retirement centers and nursing homes include a craft time in meetings or schedules because of such benefits. Though afflicted with Alzheimer's, Gerald seemed to know that creativity felt good; he often tinkered with gadgets in his workshop when he lost himself in the disease.

Perhaps the greatest benefit of developing our creativity is that it brings us closer to the heart of God. Let's see how to nurture our creativity. And no, you don't have to get out your plastic paint smock. Yet.

NURTURING CREATIVITY

Be curious. Albert Einstein said, "I have no special gift. I am only passionately curious. The important thing is not to stop questioning. Imagination is more important than knowledge." Children are experts at this, but as we age, curiosity becomes stunted or silenced by busyness, responsibility, shame or rejection. To boost creativity, ask "Why?" or "How does that work?" or "How did you learn that?" Challenge assumptions. Take an opposing viewpoint on an issue.

Reflect. Journaling jump-starts creativity, putting our life, impressions and feelings into words. As we reflect, listening to and looking at the world around us with new eyes and new ears, creativity comes alive. In addition, writing's rote hand movement reputedly frees our creative brain.

Exercise. Aerobic exercise increases creativity, possibly due to changes in brain chemistry. In addition to releasing mood-elevating endorphins, the left-right pumping of our legs limbers up the creative right brain as well, allowing the mind to free associate. New ideas, combinations and solutions stream along with increased blood flow. See what happens in twenty minutes a day.

Be spontaneous. This liberates creativity by not being afraid to play, shift gears in midstream or change plans. For the controlling person this is a hard task. Control is one of the enemies of creative living! When a handsome college graduate invited me to a banquet, my first thought was, "Absolutely not!" Then spontaneity came to my rescue and thus began the most creative adventure of my life. (I married him. See what a banquet can do? Even Queen Esther knew that.)

Laugh. Laughter is a creative, confounding life response. Stress management writer Vatche Bartekian says:

> The most productive brainstorming meetings are the ones where everyone is laughing and having a good time. The more I've watched the connection between humor and creativity, the more I've realized that there is very little difference between the terms "Aha!" and "Ha Ha!" A good laugh can be the prelude to a good idea.

Besides, laughter confounds the enemy, who prefers that gloom and doom destroy us.

Try a different route. New sights, sounds and places encourage our mind to make new creative connections. Change it up! Rearrange the starting lineup at the rink. Fold your hands the opposite way you normally do. Take the back roads home. See where you end up.

Feel your feelings. Alexander Pope said in 1717 in *Eloisa to Abelard,* "He best can paint them who shall feel them most." Clueing into the internal world enhances our creativity, clears our mind and opens us to possibility.

Grab some shut-eye. Sleep deprivation shuts down creativity and problem-solving skills.

Look again. Moses' most excellent adventure began when he turned aside to see the bush that burned but wasn't destroyed (Exodus 3:3). After a second look he shed his sandals. And the shepherd became a mighty, creative force in the freedom of an entire nation.

Like Moses, when we turn aside, when we seek the God of the burning bush, when we follow the Shepherd into places of rest, soul restoration results in creative living. As you move to that resting place now, may God breathe new life into your soul and open your eyes to his creative work within you and through you.

FOR YOUR RETREAT

Quotes to Contemplate

It is a great help in our quest to have high aspirations,
because often our actions begin with our thoughts and dreams.
It is not pride to have great desires.
It is the devil who makes us think
that the lives and actions of the saints
are to be admired but not imitated.
If we do not limit our spiritual goals,
we can with great confidence, little by little,
reach those heights that by the grace of God
many saints have reached.
If they had never resolved to desire,
and had never, little by little, acted upon that resolve,
they would never have ascended so high.

Like them we need to be humble but bold in our pursuit,
trusting God and not ourselves.
For our Lord seeks and loves courageous souls.
Let us not fail to reach our spiritual destiny
because we have been too timid, too cautious in our desires,

because we sought too little.

It is true that I might stumble for trying to do too much too soon,
but it is also certain that I will never succeed if I hope for too little
or, out of fear of failing, start not at all.

TERESA OF ÁVILA, *LET NOTHING DISTURB YOU*

A large part of living creatively is reaching outside your self to help
someone else. Learning to listen helps creative living. Listening may be
second only to loving as a creative act.

GLADYS HUNT, "LIVING CREATIVELY"

If a student flunks once, he is out; but an inventor is almost always
failing—he tries and fails maybe a thousand times. These two things are
diametrically opposite. Our biggest job is to teach how to fail intelligently
. . . to keep on trying and failing and trying.

CHARLES FRANKLIN KETTERING

A man or woman without hope in the future cannot live creatively in the
present.

HENRI J. M. NOUWEN, *OUT OF SOLITUDE*

Every child is an artist. The problem is how to remain an artist once he
grows up.

PABLO PICASSO

Meditate on Scripture

Let the favor of the Lord our God be upon us;
And confirm for us the work of our hands;
Yes, confirm the work of our hands. (Psalm 90:17 NASB)

Now the dwelling of God is with men, and he will live with them. They will be his people, and God himself will be with them and be their God. He will wipe every tear from their eyes. There will be no more death or mourning or crying or pain, for the old order of things has passed away.

He who was seated on the throne said, "I am making everything new!" (Revelation 21:3-4)

"I am the LORD; that is my name!
   I will not give my glory to another
   or my praise to idols.
See, the former things have taken place,
   and new things I declare;
before they spring into being
   I announce them to you."

Sing to the LORD a new song,
   his praise from the ends of the earth,
you who go down to the sea, and all that is in it,
   you islands, and all who live in them. (Isaiah 42:8-10)

Forget the former things;
   do not dwell on the past.
See, I am doing a new thing!
   Now it springs up; do you not perceive it?
I am making a way in the desert
   and streams in the wasteland. (Isaiah 43:18-19)

Whatever you do, work at it with all your heart, as working for the Lord, not for men, since you know that you will receive an inheritance from the Lord as a reward. It is the Lord Christ you are serving. (Colossians 3:23-24)

In the beginning God created the heavens and the earth. Now the earth was formless and empty, darkness was over the surface of the deep, and the Spirit of God was hovering over the waters.

And God said, "Let there be light," and there was light. God saw that the light was good. . . .

Then God said, "Let us make man in our image, in our likeness." . . .

So God created man in his own image,
in the image of God he created him;
male and female he created them.

God blessed them and said to them, "Be fruitful . . ." (Genesis 1:1-4, 26-28)

Journal Your Thoughts

Free your right brain today! Journal longhand, whatever comes to mind as you consider creativity. How is it operating in your life? Where do you feel dull and uncreative? Where do you feel connected to your Creator? Don't censor your soul as you journal!

Respond in Prayer

Sin hinders creativity. Pause, inviting the Holy Spirit to convict you of any hidden sins, and confess them. Take time to move into praise and thanksgiving before laying your petitions at the foot of the cross.

Consider Creation

Let the creativity of the Creator inspire you. Invite God to remove the veil and show you the glory of the world around.

Seek Stillness

In silence we move into God's creative, sustaining, loving presence. May God envelop you in the stillness.

Reflection Questions

Our fragile birthright of creativity is easily snuffed out in childhood. What messages did you receive or perceive about creativity while growing up? How impractical it is (e.g., that you should always color within the lines)? How and by whom was creativity nurtured in you?

Where do you see creativity operating in your life now? What do you see as one of your greatest hindrances to living creatively?

What relationships energize you and spark your creativity? How can you enhance current relationships and seek out new friendships that encourage your creative involvement in life?

What do you think about creativity and masculinity? femininity? How do you long to express yourself creatively in your professional life? your home? your relationships?

Consider your journey and God's presence in your life. Where do you see God "doing a new thing": redeeming past pain, creating life out of death, allowing you to love others because of where you have been?

Hymn of Praise

"Praise to the Lord, the Almighty"

Praise to the Lord, the Almighty, the King of creation!

O my soul, praise Him, for He is thy health and salvation!
All ye who hear, Now to His temple draw near;
Join me in glad adoration.

Praise to the Lord, who o'er all things so wondrously reigneth,
Shelters thee under His wings, yea, so gently sustaineth!
Hast thou not seen How thy desires e'er have been
Granted in what He ordaineth?

Praise to the Lord, who doth prosper thy work and defend thee;
Surely His goodness and mercy here daily attend thee.
Ponder anew what the Almighty can do,
If with His love He befriend thee.

JOACHIM NEANDER, 1680; TRANS. CATHERINE WINKWORTH, 1863

Examen of Conscience

As night falls, invite God to accompany you through this day. Where do you
see creativity applied, developing? Where was this gift clamped down during your day? By whom? Close the time committing your artist's soul to God,
asking for healing for the wounds of the day, forgiveness for the places where
you lost God's presence, and a tighter relationship with the Creator of the
universe.

7 & HOLY SMOKES

Finding Redemption in Anger

After church, my son and I swung into the grocery and found a steal on cereal. He chose those cereals he most liked—that is, the ones with 95 percent of calories from sugar—and we rolled to the checkout.

When the cashier scanned everything, the total seemed high. "How much did the cereal ring up?" I asked. Examining the tape, she said, "$4.95 a box." I blew up. Quietly, of course. "This happens all the time. You mark the shelves at a sale price and then key it in at a markup. This is deceitful. I don't want to shop here anymore."

"Would you like to speak to the manager?"

"Yes. This is inexcusable." I wasn't shouting, but you'd think I'd had a thousand milligrams of caffeine for breakfast and my child had just been blackballed from a team for wearing the wrong color shoe laces or that I was railing against a gross injustice like land mines in Third World countries.

The manager was calm, pacifying. The store clerk panted after running to the cereal aisle to check on prices, with the news that the shelves were properly labeled and we had misread the tags. The cereal really did cost almost an hour's minimum wage pay—per box.

Let's get this straight. I was in a lather—about cereal.

Later, I confessed to my husband, "I wasn't very nice at the store today."

"Did something at church upset you?"

Bull's-eye. My anger wasn't about being inconvenienced at the grocery store; my feelings of invalidation just surfaced there.

AN EARFUL OF ANGER

Once when I was little, a bunch of us neighborhood kids played in a friend's backyard. Suddenly he ran past me, making gagging, panicky noises. He tipped his head so one ear nearly lay on his shoulder, the other pointing straight at the sky like a satellite dish. Somehow a bird had managed to drop a load of waste straight into his ear.

Talk about an earful! In much the same manner, our anger lets loose before we even know what we're doing and we've given someone an earful of damaging words.

Anger is one of the unmentionables, a feeling relegated to the "pretend it doesn't exist" stash of untouchable subjects. We dump it, stuff it, hide it, sleep with it, coddle it—do everything except deal with it. Sometimes we don't even recognize anger as it slips into our hearts as sarcasm or sharp laughter or brittleness or depression. Ignored, anger becomes a wound of unfelt feelings and pain. It lodges within our souls, bitter as an aspirin, forming a barrier between our heart and God, our heart and others.

In addition to spiritual and relational issues, anger unchecked can result in physical problems. Angry people tend toward shorter lifespans than people who resolve their anger. According to Duke University anger specialist Dr. Redford Williams, cynicism, anger and aggression are three aspects of hostility linked to higher mortality rates. One study showed that "people who regularly quashed their anger were more than twice as likely to die in the next 12 years as people who recognized and expressed angry feelings."

Anger is good. It is a sign that we are alive and paying attention, and that we are interested in relationships. If we had no relationships, we wouldn't hold our anger.

So, then, why don't we express our anger appropriately? Why do we allow it to create distance in our relationships with self, God and others? As you move into this resting place with God, ask the Holy Spirit to lead you into a better understanding of your relationship with anger, your own soul and God.

ANGER AND SIN

Maybe we don't notice anger until it foams up in outrage or a tongue-lashing. Anger is closely associated with fear, perhaps because we have seen others use anger dangerously. It is forbidden in families like Teresa's, who said, "We have to look perfect" in order to be good or safe. Paul grew up around rage and decided that anger is never acceptable. But anger hidden or tamped down is like closing wood-boring bees inside a shed: they will drill their way through and escape to sting.

Rather than being stung or stinging others with unexpressed or poorly expressed anger, we can rethink our anger. It doesn't have to be sinful; it doesn't have to disrupt our relationships, but can enhance them. This is a God-given emotion, a feeling that God displays throughout Scripture and advises us on its management. The psalmist tells us:

> In your anger do not sin;
>> when you are on your beds,
>> search your hearts and be silent. (Psalm 4:4)

Perhaps this is one secret to anger: when we sit with it on our beds, when we let God search our hearts, we will unearth its root. But this hot-blooded emotion often rushes through with an adrenaline-like surge that surprises us and hurts others.

Anger doesn't begin as sin. It morphs into sin when it hurts us or another, when we use it to establish power or authority or control, when we wield it as a weapon in self-protection, fear or hurt. Anger becomes toxic when stored within. It contaminates its container, like mold in a clay pot. Ecclesiastes 7:9 says, "Anger resides in the lap of fools." Anger becomes sin when we attack people rather than problems, when we blame the past to excuse the present, when we accept and excuse a surly disposition or blowups as "just the way I am." It also becomes sin when we ignore it.

The 1970s birthed T-shirt philosophy. One of my brother's shirts said, "I don't get mad. I get even." We laughed in a cool '70s way, but anger is slippery, a master of disguises, and often looks like depression, resentment, unforgiveness, fatigue (from gritting your teeth and rehashing the day's indignation), irritability, control, sarcasm, inappropriate laughter, passivity, physical abuse and fury. Rage is more popular than ever: just for starters, we have road rage, cubicle rage, web rage and sports rage. We use the word *anger* to mean all sorts of feelings.

But some would tell us that anger is never appropriate, like a Sunday school teacher or uncle saying, "Never get angry. Only God displays righteous anger," as in, Jesus-cleansing-the-temple-style indignation. The reasoning goes that since we aren't righteous, we can't have righteous anger. Logically, then, we decide that Christians can't be angry yet without sin.

Nice people shouldn't get angry, and certainly not Christians. But I do get angry, so I must be a failure as a Christian. Shame rolls in on anger's heels, unless we return to the thought that anger is built into our systems by God, part of the spectrum of the heart's capabilities.

THE ROOT OF ANGER

When I think of the various situations when I have felt angry during the past month—OK, the past day or two—I was upset when someone set gym shoes on the kitchen counter. I was angry when someone was ugly to me, and when I saw a males-only board running an organization and all the committees, but with women supplying the fuel, moving into the community and actually getting programs going that met felt needs. I was angry at the political climate in our country, at the constant illness in a friend's family, at the outrageous taxes we pay in our area, at the brokenness of someone I love, and at Adam and Eve for creating such havoc in our lives.

Isn't this the gist of our anger? Our heart's deepest longing is for Eden, for safety, for a love that will never hurt or abandon us. We hunger for both respect and appreciation. The common thread running through my tacky, buckshot examples of anger is a cry for respect, safety and love. I want a perfect world!

Anger originates in a place deep within where we have forgotten, disconnected from or never known God's love for us, where others have implied either by words or actions that we aren't worth loving. Solomon's words again form a heart refrain: "What a man desires is unfailing love" (Proverbs 19:22).

Anger is the heart's cry to be well and truly loved. Might this be the root of God's anger as well? We were made for love, and God wants to love us completely, but sin gets in the way.

Righteous anger cries, "It's not fair." When my children griped like this, I stopped them with a tight, little pursed smile and said, "We won't talk like that. We can't change anything."

Now I admit, sadly, "Life isn't fair. It breaks God's heart. He didn't want it to be this way. He designed us for perfect love and beauty. That's why we need Jesus. That's why we want heaven so much."

Anger is our soul's wailing for heaven.

Anger recognizes the injustice of living in a broken world, of being loved only half-heartedly, of being inevitably hurt by those who profess to love us. This is not self-pity unless we excuse ourselves of responsibility for living well, despite the rupture of sin.

At its deepest level, anger is a healthy emotion, intended to lead us toward wholeness, righteousness, rightness with God. This is good. Unless we are angry with God.

ANGER, GRIEF AND GOD

One root word for anger is the Old Norse *angr*, which means "grief." Anger is a natural stage in grief recovery. Unlike most other early stages of grief, anger provides energy, so staying angry is easier than working through the grief, processing the underlying pain. Chronic anger may camouflage arrested grief.

And grief doesn't just have to mean the death of a loved one. Grief encompasses all loss—a lost child or a lost childhood, a lost relationship or health, job loss or financial loss, or the loss of a home. Often, digging deeper, we uncover anger at God. Because, if God allows such difficulties, maybe God doesn't really love us. Maybe God really isn't a good God, after all. Bet you weren't supposed to say that as a kid. We shouldn't even think it, should we? To wonder if God maybe doesn't love us and maybe isn't good? When we flail about with questions like these, we move a bit closer to the longings of our heart. To be well and truly loved.

The Scriptures record many examples of people being angry with God. Not that God has done anything wrong; our anger is based on a limited understanding of what God is really trying to accomplish in our lives. Jonah 4 revealed Jonah's anger at God; Elijah targeted God with his anger after a round of spiritual warfare left him depleted and standing at the mouth of a cave, mouthing off to God. Amazingly, God didn't pop him off but rather came and comforted him with the gentle breeze of his presence (1 Kings 19:14-21).

God's never-leaving love even in the face of our anger moves me. And makes me want to be honest about my heart. Michele Novotni and Randy Petersen write:

> Which is more respectful: telling someone how angry you are, or storming out of the house? When you repress your anger at God, it's like walking out of the relationship. You can't discuss the issues when you've turned your back. And you can't deepen your love for God when you're bottling up your feelings.

ANGER'S TOOLBOX

To deepen relationships we first must recognize anger. Often we don't realize that our teeth are locked, our jaw tight, our head throbbing, pulse pounding, fists clenched, feet stomping. We don't equate sleeplessness or depression or sarcasm or fatigue with anger, and when we do notice anger, we don't have the tools to handle it wisely.

The lyrics of the old hymn "Be Still My Soul" sound like a gentle soul shushing, like a parent cuddling a child and offering soothing, calming sounds. One tool to deal with anger is calm soul talk: God loves me, my Savior is on my side. This directly addresses that core longing to be loved and cared for.

To overcome anger we look for the wound. Because our wounds often explain our actions, we learn to listen to the cry underlying the behavior. If another is angry or irritable, rather than assuming the anger is a flame to the limp flag of our self-esteem, see it as a question: "Am I valuable? Do you love or appreciate me?" Then we can answer the core question rather than react to the behavior or words.

COOL DOWN: OTHER ANGER STRATEGIES

Just as we need a cool-down period after exercise to gradually bring our racing heart rate back to normal, we need cool-down strategies to calm our angry pulse.

Keep short lists. A big blowup over a small issue may mean that I've stockpiled the anger arsenal. My husband and I are on the road often, my trips leapfrogging his. He leaves, I leave, he returns, leaves again, I return. Consequently I don't always notice and process internal reactions. An exaggerated reaction over something small means I haven't kept a short list.

Now, I try to notice what's happening within and work through it quickly, deciding if it really is a big issue or something that I have magnified because of our separation. When noticing a niggling irritation or the tendency to distance, ask, "What am I angry about? When did this start? Do I need to act on it?" It's tempting, when we love others and don't have huge chunks of time together, to ignore the simmerings and press on, but this actually makes the pot boil more.

Use "I" statements. Others receive statements like "I felt hurt and angry when . . ." much better than accusing words like "You obviously don't love me or you wouldn't . . ." or "You're so selfish" or "You don't care" or . . . Owning our anger rather than blaming others for it detonates their reaction; they don't feel attacked, and anger's typical escalation halts.

Work it off. Exercise is a great cool down for anger. Running or walking blows off steam, if we don't chew the cud of fury the entire time, regurgitating injustices, stoking the fire in our bellies with acid. Once while attending a sick child in the hospital, I was so enraged over some shoddy treatment that I ran six flights of stairs repeatedly until my legs screamed and my heart didn't.

Journal. Try writing through anger. Rote hand movement frees mind and heart to feel. Invite God into the anger and clarify your heart. A journal is a safe container for our radioactivity.

Change of scenery. Reading (other than a book on anger) provides a breather and takes away the heavy weight we attach to the issue at hand. When I return from my book (and I don't mean next week or month), the heat has lowered and my vision cleared.

Time out. Table the anger discussion until both parties are calm again. Decide together to stop for a few minutes and to come together at an agreed-on time. Be sure to keep that contract so that the anger doesn't smolder and build again.

Lay off. Caffeine and sugar create an internal surge that may exacerbate a situation, inciting anger when normally we might be calm. I am much less explosive without the deadly duo.

Breathe. Deep, cleansing breaths restore the heart to a normal rate and stop the internal rushing.

Inventory emotional memories. Occasionally I boil over only to wonder later, *What was that about?* Sometimes the brain fires a "Fight!" missive based on a past event that faintly resembles a current situation. Once I reacted in fury to Rich, and later, sorting it out, I realized that a movement of his hand reminded me of a painful past relationship. I was actually raging at that person rather than Rich. Teaching ourself to inventory first, to consider trigger people, actions or words, and then determine our response saves energy and relationships.

Soul maintenance. Anger may flare when we've neglected ourself—fatigue, poor food choices, inadequate soul care. Fitting in time daily to listen to our inner tickings and to God minimizes angry reactions. Otherwise, it's as if we're ignoring a small child who needs attention, who then acts out in order to be heard.

REDEMPTIVE ANGER

Harnessed anger becomes a power for good in this world. Ezekiel says, "I went in bitterness and in the anger of my spirit, with the strong hand of the LORD upon me" (Ezekiel 3:14). He had a message of redemption for the Israelites.

Anger took the Pilgrims on a voyage to freedom, when they journeyed across the ocean to establish a new land. After the Holocaust, surviving Jews chanted, "Never again! Never again!" and determined to educate the world about the injustice and horror of prejudice. The entire Civil Rights Movement was sparked by Martin Luther King Jr.'s anger about the lack of equality and freedom for African Americans in the Land of Liberty.

Redeemed and directed, anger leads to healing.

THE PATHS OF RIGHTEOUSNESS

Thankfully, our emotions don't need to separate us from our Shepherd. Instead they can lead us right into God's presence, into that place where our soul is restored, our deepest longings met. In this resting place, we find the One who receives our heart and all its baggage, and loves us deeply. Our anger guides us into paths of righteousness.

FOR YOUR RETREAT

Quotes to Contemplate

A part of the quiet rage I experienced was anger against God. Inwardly and very quietly, I raved and ranted against Him in my spirit. . . . It's better to get angry at God than to walk away from Him. It's better to honestly confront our feelings and let Him know this is how we feel—this is awful, my pillow is wet from all my tears, I'm sick and tired of this, and I can't stand it one more minute.

JONI EARECKSON TADA, *DARK CLOUDS, SILVER LININGS*

When people can express harsh feelings to the One or ones who are their object, love is already stronger in them than their feelings. Love is already transforming, transfiguring, this feeling into something else, something closer to love than to hatred. The power of the Resurrection is already working in them. Perhaps there is hatred present as long as people are mute, absolutely mute; but as soon as they decide to express what is in their heart to the other, something is already changing and maybe even already changed. . . . This expression is a desire for reconciliation.

PIERRE WOLFF, *MAY I HATE GOD?*

Anger can be a response to pain, . . . when your spouse responds in anger, you must terminate the argument. It's that simple: the argument must end

because another person may be in pain. . . . When you discover the pain,
you can address its cause, and the anger will begin to fade. . . .
Dumping anger on your partner is a poor way to soothe your hurt.
When you talk about your hurt without anger, an unangry response
usually comes.

GERRY SPENCE, HOW TO ARGUE AND WIN EVERY TIME

In using our anger . . . [to determine] our innermost needs, values and
priorities, we should not be distressed if we discover just how unclear we
are. If we feel chronically angry or bitter in an important relationship, this
is a signal that too much of the self has been compromised and we are
uncertain about what new position to take or what options we have
available to us. To recognize our lack of clarity is not a weakness but an
opportunity, a challenge, and a strength. . . . It is an act of courage to
acknowledge our own uncertainty and sit with it for a while. . . . Our anger
can be a powerful vehicle for personal growth and change if it does nothing
more than help us recognize that we are not yet clear about something and
that it is our job to keep struggling with it.

HARRIET GOLDHOR LERNER, THE DANCE OF ANGER

Emotional maturity is the ability to know what it is that I am feeling, what
its name is, then to discover positive channels for it. The quicker the
process operates in us, the more mature we are becoming. Spiritual
maturity requires that we submit to this procedure before the Lord.

KAREN MAINS, KAREN! KAREN!

Meditate on Scripture

Do not be quickly provoked in your spirit,
for anger resides in the lap of fools. (Ecclesiastes 7:9)

Go ahead and be angry. You do well to be angry—but don't use your anger as fuel for revenge. And don't stay angry. Don't go to bed angry. Don't give the Devil that kind of foothold in your life. . . .

Watch the way you talk. Let nothing foul or dirty come out of your mouth. Say only what helps, each word a gift.

Don't grieve God. Don't break his heart. His Holy Spirit, moving and breathing in you, is the most intimate part of your life, making you fit for himself. Don't take such a gift for granted.

Make a clean break with all cutting, backbiting, profane talk. Be gentle with one another, sensitive. Forgive one another as quickly and thoroughly as God in Christ forgave you. (Ephesians 4:26-27, 29-32 *The Message*)

Everyone should be quick to listen, slow to speak and slow to become angry, for man's anger does not bring about the righteous life that God desires. . . .

If anyone considers himself religious and yet does not keep a tight rein on his tongue, he deceives himself and his religion is worthless. (James 1:19-20, 26)

An angry man stirs up dissension,
    and a hot-tempered one commits many sins. (Proverbs 29:22)

He who restrains his words has knowledge,
    And he who has a cool spirit is a man of understanding.
        (Proverbs 17:27 NASB)

Journal Your Thoughts

Get the anger on the outside! Try journaling through an angry reaction, either a current one or one from your past. Ask God to help you get to the heart of the anger and to guide you into a healing, helpful place with your anger.

Respond in Prayer

Anger will keep us from God if we let it. Instead, let anger take you to God, where you can share your anger, its painful origins and ask for help.

Consider Creation

The rhythm and beauty of creation put our emotions in perspective and move us into God's creative presence. If you are angry, take it outside and see what God does with you and your heart in the midst of the created order.

Seek Stillness

Invite your soul into silence, hushing your heart gently, honoring any woundings. Let God's presence rise within you, until you are in a place of deep stillness and healing peace.

Reflection Questions

In what situations do you become angry? Think through the past week. When have you felt angry? What did you do with that anger? How long did it take you to go to God with it? How did others react when you revealed your anger to them?

Pick a time when you really blew it with your anger. How did it get so big? What was your heart's hope beneath that reaction? How can you handle your anger so that it doesn't separate you from God, but also doesn't allow you to obsess about it or deny its existence?

Maybe you are thinking, *I never get angry.* Why not? What stops you from feeling anger? There are plenty of reasons for anger in this broken, fallen, imperfect world. What messages have you received that keep you from feeling this anger?

Poorly expressed anger always brings with it the possibility for repentance and forgiveness, both before God and with others. With whom is this true for you? What action do you need to take?

When has anger been a redemptive force in your life? How can anger over past pain or injustice become a tool for good?

Hymn of Praise

"Be Still My Soul"

Be still my soul: the Lord is on your side.
Bear patiently the cross of grief or pain.
Leave to your God to order and provide.
In every change God faithful will remain. . . .

Be still my soul: your God will undertake
To guide the future, as in ages past.
Your hope, your confidence let nothing shake;
All now mysterious shall be bright at last. . . .

Be still my soul: the hour is hastening on
When we shall be forever with the Lord,
When disappointment, grief and fear are gone,
Sorrow forgot, love's purest joys restored. . . .

KATHARINA VON SCHLEGEL, 1752; TRANS. JANE L. BORTHWICK, 1855

Examen of Conscience

Thankfully, we can rush boldly to the throne of grace and receive mercy when we need it. And when we are angry, we need grace and mercy. Find these in God's presence now as you go back through your day, looking for anger, woundings, inappropriate reactions. Ask for the Comforter to soothe and heal, and bring you into a whole place.

8 ❧ GET A GRIP

Learning How to Give God Control

Footsteps reverberated as we tromped up the metal stairway toward a tourist attraction. As self-appointed captain, I corralled the children with a fire hose of commands. "Hold on to the handrail. Look over there! Don't shove. Be careful." That my tour group was all related to me lent my commands credibility. They had to obey. I was kin.

Little legs (and big legs) were tired on the descent, and one of the children spied an elevator with delight. "Let's ride the elevator the rest of the way."

But no. That was not part of my plan for our sightseeing. "Nothing wrong with our legs. Good for us," I panted. "Besides, read that sign. *Use only in emergencies.*" As soon as my children walked alone, I determined to deplete their energies before strapping them into car seats. One little legalism was: Never use the elevator when stairs are present. Despite huffs, puffs and eyes rolling, down we clomped. The lecture continued, "What if we used the elevator when someone else really needed it?"

At the bottom of the stairs, a herd of boys, unsupervised, poked at the elevator button. I decided to believe the best: they didn't know how to read. In an effort toward charitable education, I said, "Hey, guys, the sign says, 'Use only in emergencies.'"

Their eyes widened with disbelief. And something else. Scorn? One boy jabbed the button again. Feeling a teeny surge of anger, I became Police Woman of the World. "Look, boys, let's be obedient . . ."

My own children shrank in embarrassment. My cousin cleared her throat and flashed dark, horrified eyes at me. Niece and nephew tried to disappear into the metal siding behind us. Ignoring them, I tried false concern, "Is this an emergency? Can I help?"

The elevator shuddered open, and the boys leaped into safety, stabbing "close" repeatedly and with desperation. As the doors slid together, I might have jumped in after them with a lesson on good citizenship if my cousin hadn't yanked me away by my elbow.

CONTROL

Why did I feel a need to control their behavior? I didn't know them, would never see them again, didn't have to pay the elevator's electric bill. Besides, what would constitute an emergency at this site? Would it be life-or-death? But I made it into a huge right versus wrong issue.

Legalism is thinly veiled control. And I was ripe with rules. The Pharisees would have declared me an honorary member.

Control: the effort to regulate—to exercise restraining or directing influence over another. My efforts at control are unrelenting and global—I try to control the clerk and the taxi driver and the politician and people in parking lots and anyone who enters my sphere.

And why did I need to control those boys? To feel superior? To buffer my self-esteem?

Yes. All of the above, no doubt. What an ideal way to alienate those I love and keep my blood pressure elevated to vein-popping levels. My control issues prevent me from trusting God as my resting place, seeking restoration and loosening my grip on the entire world.

CONTROLLERS ARISE!

Controlling people may feel powerless in other areas, felt powerless as children or grew up being handed inappropriate power. These highchair tyrants believe they have the authority and ability to bend the world to their demands. Control feels like a birthright.

For others, control secured approval. The more they did, the more affirmation they received, and the more they tried to do. Being in charge was the only way to feel safe or good about themselves.

For Lars, control surfaced everywhere but chiefly at church, serving on every strategic committee and raising his hand for every responsibility, especially finances. He oversaw every detail, including the ledgers. At a meeting, someone asked about money. He refused to release figures. He pounded the table, raised his voice, badgered the members into silence. Ultimately, they asked him to step down—and learned he had hidden the church's enormous debt from them.

Demanding that the world fit into our preconceived—and thus correct—understanding and interpretation, controllers are afraid of changes in plans, of having fun, of interruptions in their schedules.

As children we had little control over our environment or the events that took place in our lives. As adults we control our feelings and behavior, and we try to control the feelings and behaviors of others. We become rigid, manipulative, and we lack spontaneity in our lives. There is an element of distrust in our need to control. We trust only ourselves to carry out a task or to handle a situation. We manipulate others in order to manage their impressions of us, and we keep a balance that feels safe for us. We fear that our lives will get worse if we let go of control. We become stressed and anxious when control is not possible.

When my issues began shredding my family and faith, I went outside the church for help with anger, control issues, codependency. As I healed, I occasionally related a personal struggle, then floated a question in Sunday school: "So, do any of you have control issues?" Like starlings chatter when a firecracker explodes, these godly people yakked in a frenzy about control.

Our group tried to control our dates, families, colleagues, neighbors. And if we couldn't control people's actions, we tried to control their thoughts about us. We controlled by refusing to forgive, by anger or violence. Praying aloud revealed our hidden agenda for God and others.

Rarely, however, did our struggles with control include self-control. We didn't try to control ourselves, our temper, our despondency or our self-care (or lack thereof). Instead, we directed profound efforts and energies at controlling others.

A myth: that we actually have any control over other people's lives. But we continue to engage in this futile behavior. Very few of our attempts at control are fruitful, faithful or helpful.

SIDE EFFECTS OF CONTROL

All behaviors benefit us in some way. Control falsely boosts self-esteem, safety, guaranteed outcomes, authority, superiority, applause and approval. But the price is high.

If my way is the only way, controlling implies judgment and damages my relationships and my soul. Questioning a purchase, I telegraph: "You make bad choices. I don't trust you. I can't be happy for your good fortune." When I point out every mistake my children make, I'm not only exerting control in retrospect, but I communicate: "You never get it right; you are not good enough." Both instances send the message: "You are a failure."

This approach damages us as well. "I should be able to control home, family, careers, universe." Shame follows because we inevitably fail at the control panel, and stress plagues us because the job is never done. The resultant anxiety, fear, anger and stress hurt our health, keeping us churning and sleep-deprived because "If I don't do this, who will?" Surely not God.

Putting ourselves at the center of the world, setting ourselves as the supreme authority in this way seems to be the essence of our sin sickness. People with control issues need a resting place. We need to find God again.

For some, life is a constant reaction to the action of others. Someone *makes* us angry. We explode. Another's bad mood puts us in a bad mood. Someone changes the plans; we stay home or else pout while enduring the new schedule. Our students act rude; we react with rudeness. When we allow another to determine our attitudes and actions, our feelings, we allow them to control us. It's no different than a teenager knuckling under to negative peer pressure. When we return evil for evil, ugly for ugly, we give up our own control and let others choose for us.

TROLLING FOR CONTROL'S ORIGIN

Looking backward, we may locate the reason for our need for control—whether control looks like bending others to our will or becoming dependent so others must care for us. Betty controls her home by whining. Her mother controlled her home by arguing and shaming. Betty's grandmother controlled by yelling. And the cycle continues.

Peter's learned passivity got people to take care of him, beginning with his mother. His father's attempts to "make a man out of him" brought down Mamma's ire, and their battle for control sealed Peter's behavior. He sought a caretaker when dating. His passivity nearly ruined his marriage, except that he married—surprise—a woman who thrives on control, though she secretly longs to be cared for herself. Peter's learned helplessness controls the home.

What about Lars, whose controlling ran his church into debt? He needed to perform, to receive his parents' approval, to look good to others. He loved hearing "I don't know how you do it all." He gloried in feeling able to control everything and be the expert on all issues, from technology to money to the nursery ministry. But the more he took on, the less he could actually perform, so he hid the truth in fear of being discovered.

If we trace control far enough back, we'll end up in Eden, with Adam and Eve vying for control and autonomy. Sure, God said "rule"—but we take God's word *rule* way out of context and its intended realm.

SELF-CONTROL

Controlling others is more interesting than controlling myself—my mouth, my actions, my thoughts. Mary laughed at this. "I try to change the whole world and I can't change myself." Maybe that's one of the reasons we try to control the world, because we can't rein ourselves in. When I'm controlling others, I shift focus from my own sin and shortcomings. I don't have to endure painful soul-searching. I don't have to change or risk doing something wrong, because I'm so busy telling others how to do it right. I don't have to repent, seek forgiveness or make amends, because I'm not wrong. Others are.

Control is an evasion of maturity. We attempt to manipulate another's impressions or opinions of us through our actions. Including, at times, God's opinion of us. Scripture doesn't exactly invite us to exercise other-control. It highlights self-control as a Christian hallmark. Second Timothy 1:7 says, "For God did not give us a spirit of timidity, but a spirit of power, of love and of self-discipline." One of the fruits of the Spirit is self-control (Galatians 5:22-23). Titus mentions self-control five times. Lack of self-control was ruining their witness, making them blend in with unbelievers. Self-control isn't only about what we don't do, it's also about what we do. Paul says repeatedly in Titus, "Do what is good."

Self-control seems an impossibility at best or a misnomer. I can't get a grip by my own efforts. Self-control comes only when I relinquish control to God and invite the Holy Spirit to control me and my world again, when I acquiesce to God's sovereignty.

THE WHITE FLAG

The sunrise blazed into our bedroom. But I had been awake, again, almost all night. Worries ran rampant in my brain. Life was beyond my control, and I could not trust God. Exhaustion wore me down until I had to give in. Before swinging my legs over the edge of the bed, I said, "I give up, Lord." Then I worked my way through my worries: my children, my past, my fear of the future, my expectations and disappointments. As I gave up control, God began to move again in my heart and in my family.

The only way out of the shaming cycle of fear and control is surrender. "I can't control my desire to control everyone and everything. It's killing me and everyone I love." We get a grip on control by opening our hands and replacing fear with its faith-filled opposite—trust. Only God brings our life under control. Recognizing the insanity of our need to control, the desire for freedom lurches and stumbles to life within us like a newborn colt trying out brand new legs.

What irony that as we give up control, we find it. We confuse control with strength and surrender with weakness, when the reverse is true. When we die to our desire to run the world, we come into real power. God's power. Real freedom lies in trusting God.

This is not a once-for-all decision, but sometimes a minute-by-minute one, when we relinquish our hunger for control and turn back to God. When we wave our white flag of surrender. Again and again we hand the remote control to God.

Worry is about control or the lack of it, and control is about fear, about not trusting that God will care for us. We are not our own bottom line, thankfully. God is. God has promised to be our keeper, the shade at our right hand. God has pledged to hold us in his palm and never forsake us. God has assured us to act in our best interests, even when it doesn't look like it from our puny vantage point.

Rest isn't just the act of sleeping, of lying prone, of ceasing movement. It implies inner stillness and trust, which come from allowing another to be in charge. Rest means renouncing control.

THE SURRENDERED LIFE

Living as if the spinning of the world depended on us is living in denial of Christ's life surrendered for us. He laid down his life, that we might take up his life. Controllers either make their own laws or try scrupulously to live by God's law and secure approval and acceptance from others. But Galatians 2:19-20 reads, "For through the law I died to the law so that I might live for God. I have been crucified with Christ and I no longer live, but Christ lives in me. The life I live in the body, I live by faith in the Son of God, who loved me and gave himself up for me."

Christ surrendered his godhood, his rights, his very life to dwell on earth as human flesh, then surrendered that flesh on a cross. Clinging to imaginary control denies that truth.

"Why do you do this?" Jesus asks, tenderly. "I uphold the whole world. I care for your loved ones more than you dream possible. I love you beyond anything you can ask or imagine. I'll take care of the outcome of everything. Loosen your grip. You don't have to clench the world in the palm of your hand. I already have them, securely, in my own."

And when I can trust that hand enough, I reach out my own hand and grasp his.

May the Shepherd lead you into the fullness that life offers, a place where fear is banned and rest is real. And you can dwell in the house of the Lord forever, and moment by moment, as well.

For Your Retreat

Quotes to Contemplate

When we don't like ourselves, we need to change others; when we like ourselves, we don't need to fix anyone.

CECIL MURPHEY

Let go and let God surprise you.

GINNEY TUCKER

The end of our control . . . is the beginning of God's reign.

KATHLEEN NORRIS, *THE CLOISTER WALK*

In experiences of solitude we gently press into the Holy of Holies, where we are sifted in the stillness. Painfully, we let go of the vain images of ourselves in charge of everything and everybody. Slowly, we loosen our grip on all those projects that to us seem so significant. Gently, we become more focused and simplified. Joyfully, we receive the nourishment of heavenly manna.

RICHARD FOSTER, *PRAYER*

As we relinquish control and admit weaknesses, we remember who we are and why we're here. The sun does not rise and set on our achievements, but on the love of God. Life is a journey of coming to know God, not achieving or gaining others' approval. . . . Letting go is both too simple and too difficult. It looks like weakness instead of strength, like losing instead of gaining, and it is. . . . Responding to God's call to surrender forces me to value my brokenness, as well as my strength.

JAN JOHNSON, "THE VIRTUE OF SURRENDER," VIRTUE

Letting go does not mean to stop caring;
It means I can't do it for someone else.
Letting go is not to cut myself off;
It's the realization that I can't control another.
Letting go is not to enable;
But to allow learning from natural consequences.
Letting go is to admit powerlessness;
Which means the outcome is not in my hands.
Letting go is not to try to change or blame another;
It's to make the most of myself.
Letting go is not to care for; but to care about.
Letting go is not to fix; but to be supportive.
It's not to judge but to allow another to be a human being.
Letting go is not to be in the middle arranging the outcome;
But to allow others to affect their own destinies.
Letting go is not to be protective;
It's to permit another to face reality.
Letting go is not to deny, but to accept.
Letting is not to nag, scold, or argue;
But to search out my own shortcomings and correct them.
Letting go is not to adjust everything to my desires;
But to take each day as it comes and cherish myself in it.
Letting go is not to criticize and regulate anybody;

But to try to become what I dream I can be.
Letting go is to not regret the past;
But to grow and live for the future.
Letting go is to fear less and live more.

AUTHOR UNKNOWN

Meditate on Scripture

In him we live and move and have our being. (Acts 17:28)

In the past God spoke to our forefathers through the prophets at many times and in various ways, but in these last days he has spoken to us by his Son, whom he appointed heir of all things, and through whom he made the universe. The Son is the radiance of God's glory and the exact representation of his being, sustaining all things by his powerful word. (Hebrews 1:1-3)

I can do everything through him who gives me strength. (Philippians 4:13)

Finally, be strong in the Lord and in his mighty power. (Ephesians 6:10)

But the fruit of the Spirit is love, joy, peace, patience, kindness, goodness, faithfulness, gentleness and self-control. Against such things there is no law. Those who belong to Christ Jesus have crucified the sinful nature with its passions and desires. Since we live by the Spirit, let us keep in step with the Spirit. (Galatians 5:22-25)

Journal Your Thoughts

Take inventory of your control issues. Where are you most likely to control others? What happens when you do? Where are you tempted toward passivity? Recognizing the times when we are most susceptible helps us pray and plan how to relinquish control in those places.

Respond in Prayer

Prayer is sometimes an attempt to control God, clarifying our agenda, our desires, our goals. Instead of trying to tell God what to do, ask for clarity of God's desires. Confession, praise, petition: these, done with a whole heart, are examples of relaxing our grip and trusting God.

Consider Creation

Trust is inherent in nature. Trees don't try to grow. Flowers don't try to bloom. They just do their job and growth results. What other lessons might God be trying to impart as you observe the created world?

Seek Stillness

Being still—silent—ceasing striving—in God's presence reminds us that we have *no* control. In our silent bowing we give up control and find that we are free.

Reflection Questions

How does control show up for you? In what relationship(s) do you most struggle to be in charge (e.g., in your family of origin)? What is the root of your controlling?

What techniques do you use to control others: shame, anger, withdrawal, unforgiveness, dependency?

How do you react to changes and interruptions over which you have no control? To what extent do you allow others to determine your reaction, giving up control?

What do you gain by control or other-controlling or passivity? How does control affect you? How does it affect others? Where have you seen the cost of being controlling or lack of self-control or passivity?

Letting go or giving up seems ridiculous, even insane at times. What is your greatest fear? When we let go, we find that Someone greater has us in hand. When have you experienced this?

Hymn of Praise

"I Surrender All"

All to Jesus I surrender;
All to him I freely give;
I will ever love and trust him,
In his presence daily live.

All to Jesus I surrender;
Humbly at his feet I bow,
Worldly pleasures all forsaken;
Take me Jesus, take me now.

All to Jesus I surrender;
Make me, Savior, wholly Thine;
Let me feel the Holy Spirit,
Truly know that thou art mine.

All to Jesus I surrender;
Lord, I give myself to Thee;
Fill me with Thy love and power,
Let Thy blessing fall on me.

JUDSON W. VAN DEVENTER, 1896

Examen of Conscience

Invite God's presence as you close this day. Take stock of your waking hours. Where did you sense the Holy Spirit controlling and leading you, speaking to and through you? When did you wrestle with control? self-control? Ask God's healing for wounds you endured, wounds you gave, and feel God's blessing and forgiveness and grace.

9 ✑ MONEY MADNESS

Discovering the Riches Stored Up for You

Last year's journals revealed an inescapable pattern. The ink, poured out over money worries, condemned me.[2]

Who knew when we moved into this new ministry that money would break my spiritual bank account? Fear gnawed daily: how we would eat, cover the mortgage, even buy gas to get to speaking or worship events?

Fear didn't only chew on me; it spread through our family like the stomach flu. I snapped, nagged, interrupted and otherwise tried to control my husband and three children. Buying milk only to spot it elsewhere for two cents less panicked me. I drove on empty on the highway for miles, children nibbling their nails, because someone down the road surely sold gas more cheaply.

Check the math. If I saved even a nickel per gallon of gas, with a sixteen-gallon tank, we were talking about ninety cents. No doubt the agony and risks were worth it.

So in January I decided not to worry incessantly about money. Checking my current journal, I counted only five references to money. In the first five entries.

I don't think that's progress.

---

[2]Portions of this chapter first appeared in "From Fear to Fasting: A Lesson in God's Faithfulness," *Indeed*, July/August 2005, pp. 9-10. *Indeed* is published by Walk Thru the Bible Ministries. Used by permission.

MONEY MADNESS

Money fuels more fights and raises more hackles between husbands and wives than nearly any other subject. Raise the subject of money and church boards broil. Propose hiking taxes for a school referendum and citizens gird their loins.

We've lost our perspective, overinflating money's meaning, overlooking its powerful emotional hold. Our possessions become paramount, as though net worth determines our self-worth.

With 600 million credit cards in circulation and an average of $7,000 in credit card debt, consumers max out their current cards and then open up new accounts. Household debt for the average family stands at 93 percent of annual disposable income, with an estimated $800 billion owed. Americans earn more than ever, yet gain less satisfaction from their money.

Whether money makes us mad, manic or moody, it packs a psychological and emotional wallop. More importantly, my attitude about money is a gauge of my heart before God. Money worries and rest are mutually exclusive. Does money become my resting place?

Unpacking the meaning of money can change our lives.

THE MEANING OF MONEY

Jesus mentioned money more than any other subject; sixteen of his thirty-eight parables deal with money. He changed a money-lover's heart (Matthew, the tax collector), dumped the money-changers' coffers, lauded the widow whose last cent went into the offering, and told us, "You cannot serve God and mammon" (Matthew 6:24 NASB). And "Do not store up for yourselves treasures on earth" (Matthew 6:19). He told the rich young man who asked about inheriting eternal life and who had kept all of God's commandments, "Go, sell everything you have and give to the poor, and you will have treasure in heaven. Then come, follow me" (Mark 10:21). The guy went away very sad. Our treasures end up owning us, and Jesus knew it.

Our spending reveals our priorities. A woman with red sculptured nails (upkeep: $50 per month, minimum) passed the offering basket and dropped in a single. There's nothing wrong with sculptured nails (until you try to get them off). What do our spending habits demonstrate about our relationship with God and with ourselves? With all of the gleaming late-model cars in church parking lots, what are we really worshiping, and how much interest do we pay for the privilege?

Faithfulness demands that we address money's grip on us. What are we trying to buy with our money?

SAFETY, SELF-ESTEEM AND POWER

The great mystique—and myth—of Mammon is that it can purchase us safety, self-esteem and power.

Safety. Money procured safety for Vera: she could support her children if her husband failed her. Buying safety is not unique. In the Old Testament the Israelites were frequently the target of the much larger and wealthier surrounding countries. Often the Hebrew kings, rather than rely on God's power and protection, taxed the people heavily and sent the tribute money to other countries, supposedly securing safety.

What they really secured was enslavement to the foreign rulers, the very thing from which the Lord had delivered them in Egypt.

With our devotion to buying, how different are we from the Israelites? Does our willingness to pay 18 to 25 percent interest demonstrate a slavish need for safety?

Self-esteem. After her divorce, Lynda salved her misery with credit cards; her purchases helped her feel desirable again. Ben needed the props of affluence to cover a chronic sense of inferiority, and he destroyed his marriage and saddled his whole family with debt.

Beneath the love affair with money and buying hides the hope that money can buy us love (contrary to the Beatles' lyrics). Seeking our worth, not in our income or what it can buy, but in the imperishable love of God, is the only way we will ever find safety and acceptance.

Power. When cheap became chic, the frugality wave of the 1990s swept me under with its subtle message of power. Saving money meant that the advertising execs and their trickery did not sway me. Becoming master of what moolah we had nurtured the neurotic in me and created a self-righteous pride in my ability to deny myself and take up my cross.

For many, though, the opposite side of money and power attracts. More money equals more power. With enough money, we can buy up competitors, obliterate enemies, snag votes, offices, corporations. We can wield our wealth for good, of course. Money helps with hunger, medical care, housing, insurance. Because it does have the power to make life easier, it's easy to assume that money can make us feel better about our losses or buy us revenge if another has "done us wrong."

This power creates its own problems even while solving some basic life requirements. How do you know if you are loved for yourself or for your money? Do others respect you or your yen, your character or the things your bucks can buy?

Of all the commandments the most overlooked one may be "You shall not covet" (Exodus 20:17). God orders us not to envy our neighbor's spouse, house, slave or income—in fact, anything. Not their lawn mower or car or new snow blower. Not their rec room or their perfect children or their fancy vacations.

Coveting builds our culture. Commercials promise that by spending a little (or a lot), we can be beautiful, sporty, macho, cool, rich, powerful, athletic, admired, sexy, powerful. All this and white teeth too. The media is designed to make us want.

Our wants take us out of God's hand. As if God doesn't have any understanding of our needs and desires or what is best for us. Taking our eyes off God as our Provider creates fertile soil for the seeds of discontent.

A Soul Gap

Discontent—that desire for bigger, better, more or different—should alert us to our tendency to use the visible to medicate, numb, distract or fill up. Temptation stalks us to use people or power or possessions to fill the great gulf in our souls, which can be filled only with God's presence. "Keep your lives free from the love of money and be content with what you have, because God has said, 'Never will I leave you; / never will I forsake you'" (Hebrews 13:5). And Jesus said, "All the nations worry about food and clothing. Don't keep worrying. Your heavenly Father knows you need this stuff. Just seek the kingdom. These things will be taken care of" (Luke 12:29-31, my paraphrase).

In our hustle-bustle—get an education, make a good living, go into debt—rat race, we have no idea what Jesus meant: "Do not be afraid, little flock, for your Father has chosen gladly to give you the kingdom" (Luke 12:32 NASB). The kingdom! Jesus' words affect me deeply when I remember that it took his death on a cross to assure me that gift.

In Deuteronomy 6, God warns the Israelites as they prepare to move into their new land, filled with houses and gardens and wells. God knew they would idolize their current belongings and forget the One providing those gifts. God rescued them from slavery, delighted to give them a homeland, knowing the danger: they would return to slavery by means of their possessions.

Jesus understood the risk of laying up treasures on earth, of worshiping our wallets or what our money (or plastic) can buy.

"Beware, and be on your guard against every form of greed; for not even when one has an abundance does his life consist of his possessions" (Luke 12:15 NASB). The temptation is twofold: to assume that life is what we see, and that we have brought it about in the first place.

The Israelites lived in an agrarian society, knowing the intimate connection between God, weather and harvest. When we nonfarmers receive a paycheck, we actually believe we earned it. Our work is simply the conduit, the means by which God delivers our livelihood. When work or our employer acts as the middleman, we are easily blinded to our total dependence on our Lord. God provides whatever we do have, whether it comes in the form of a paycheck or a bushel of wheat. Paul told Timothy to remind people to put their hope "in God, who richly provides us with everything for our enjoyment" (1 Timothy 6:17).

MONEY AND GOD

My anxiety with money forces me to examine my faith. What do I believe about God? What if God isn't going to cover us in this ministry? Maybe we use different calculators. Maybe our mortgage—or the school fees or the electric bill—isn't important to God. Maybe God isn't a good God.

Maybe, in fact, God doesn't really love us and is playing a cruel game to shake us off the team. I cringe. The Surgeon is probing a damaged nerve. How much of our money madness is related to our longing to be loved? To know we are valuable and valued, precious sons and daughters of the Most High? And when the checkbook doesn't show a healthy surplus, when the car is rusted, when we lose our job or curb our lifestyle to shorten the gap between means and ends, it's easy to believe that God must not love us and that in fact God highly esteems the people around us who have all the trappings of power, possessions and status.

When I was worrying, again, about our finances, my covenant group listened closely, lovingly. And one of them asked, kindly, "Jane, where are you living? In the house of money? Or the house of God?"

"Abide in me," Jesus stated.

Regardless of what is stamped on our coins, in whom do we really trust when it comes to our money? And whose money is it, anyway?

MAMMON AND AN ETERNITY MINDSET

"God keeps his money in your pockets," a guest preacher exclaimed. I'm not sure how much we believe this, given statistics: "The average donation by adults who attend U.S. Protestant churches is about $17 a week." If it isn't ours to start with, wouldn't knowing that everything we have comes from God change our grip on money?

Though growing up poor, Cleo has a different relationship with money than many with a similar background. Money never rescued her—Jesus did. She knows the value of money and of using it to influence eternity. Friends gave her a certificate to an expensive salon; she returned with the perfect hairstyle. Everyone raved.

"I don't understand all this fuss over my hair. That $150 could have helped keep three teens in Christian rehab for a month. In ten years it would still reap benefits in their lives. I don't want to put the money on my head. I want to put it into heaven and people's hearts."

One couple downsized, weary of the drain of time and money for upkeep on their custom home. "We're freeing up our resources for the kingdom." These people take seriously Jesus' story of the nobleman who gave his servants money, instructing them to "put this money to work . . . until I come back" (Luke 19:13). Looking at money's effect on eternity sets us free.

Consider John Wesley's words: "Earn all you can, save all you can, give all you can." Where do you stand given that advice?

Money becomes our god when it dominates our emotions, preoccupies our heart, controls our mind and rules our relationships. When we give away our money, it no longer controls us.

MASTERING MAMMON

Bookwork consumed the weekend. Three months since our last regular paycheck; five years since depositing money in savings. A Mother Hubbard kitchen. Bills piled up three inches high. So I followed my instincts. Chew, chew, chew. I carried my autoimmune tendency to church with me, continuing to let my fears try to kill me off one cell at a time. Elemental conflict engaged me: Where is my treasure? Who am I serving?

In the service we embraced Psalm 117.

Praise the LORD, all you nations;
    extol him, all you peoples.
For great is his love toward us,
    and the faithfulness of the LORD endures forever.
Praise the LORD.

The entire chapter pointed to God's faithfulness and our response: praise.

God's love is great and God cannot *not* be faithful. I ducked my head and mentally reviewed the ledger: five-plus years of this ministry. Our clothes haven't worn out. Our cars are worn but (usually) running. We have little debt. None of us is losing weight from privation. We are following God's call with our gifts. Praise bubbled up and tears leaked out. The pressure on my chest lessened.

Later, worries descended again, even after my Bible-in-a-year reading included Philippians 4:19: "my God shall meet all your needs according to his glorious riches in Christ Jesus." Intellectually I believed that to be true. Practically, I preferred to worry.

REAL HUNGER

I decided to put this fear to the hunger test. Fasting for a day, every time my stomach rumbled, I would pray that God would meet people's needs through us and meet our needs however he chose.

This was about my inability to be God. This was about God's riches, not mine; about rejoicing in the Lord, whose love endures forever, which gives me plenty to celebrate.

This is not about expenses versus income. This is about God. When I felt hunger just now, I rested my head on my desk. "Oh God. You have everything we need." My brain did a jolt. "You *are* everything we need. In you, we have everything."

Hunger rings an old bell, reminding me that my deepest hunger is not relief from monetary pressures but to be well and truly loved. Only God can do that. And in the meantime he can take care of all my petty problems with Mammon.

THE PATH OF RIGHTEOUSNESS

If this is not so, then, what does Psalm 23:1 mean? "The LORD is my shepherd; / I shall not want." Others translate it: "I shall not be in need," or "I shall lack nothing." Can we take that literally? Or does it mean, we will lack nothing life or death? Like Maslow's hierarchy of needs, where the most crucial things top the list and the nice things like affirmation land somewhere in the "It would be great if possible but you won't die without 'em" section?

In the context of the psalmist's words, wherever we are with money—deprivation, debt, no savings, slaving to make ends meet, filled with fear or flush with paychecks or posh pension—somehow this is to lead us to godliness. Because David goes on in verse 3, "He guides me in the paths of righteousness / for his name's sake." Why do I wait around and worry, then? Why not take the anxiety, longing, money mistakes, hope and fear, to the One with a plan and a purpose?

We will never find our safety, our self-esteem, our power or purpose in silver and gold. Money really can't buy us love, which sets us free to punch out and keep that date with the Shepherd. His smile is as bright as the sunshine, more brilliant than a newly minted coin.

When God is our resting place, we can dwell not in the house of money but in the house of the Lord. Forever.

FOR YOUR RETREAT

Quotes to Contemplate

Our prosperity has camouflaged our spiritual poverty.

LLOYD OGILVIE

*We cling to our possessions rather than sharing them because we are
anxious about tomorrow. But if we truly believe that God is who Jesus said
He is, then we do not need to be afraid.*

RICHARD FOSTER, CELEBRATION OF DISCIPLINE

*There are people who use up their entire lives making money so they can
enjoy the lives they have entirely used up.*

*Jesus says it's easier for a camel to go through the eye of a needle than
for a rich man to enter the Kingdom of God. Maybe the reason is not that
the rich are so wicked they're kept out of the place, but that they're so out
of touch with reality they can't see it's a place worth getting into.*

FREDERICK BUECHNER, BEYOND WORDS

*But if thou art poor, then look not on thy purse when it is empty. He who
desires more than God wills him to have, is also a servant of Mammon, for
he trusts in what God has made, and not in God Himself. He who laments*

what God has taken from him, he is a servant of Mammon. He who for care cannot pray, is a servant of Mammon.

GEORGE MACDONALD, *PAUL FABER, SURGEON*

Often people attempt to live their lives backward: they try to have more things, or more money, in order to do more of what they want so that they will be happier. The way it actually works is the reverse. You must first be who you really are, then, do what you need to do, in order to have what you want.

MARGARET YOUNG

To give away money is to win a victory over the dark powers that oppress us. [We must] reclaim for ourselves the energy with which we have endowed money: "Money is a hang-up for many of us. We will not be able to advance in the Christian faith until we have dealt at another level with the material [world]. It is a matter of understanding what it means to be faithful to Jesus Christ."

ELIZABETH O'CONNOR, QUOTING GORDON COSBY IN *LETTERS TO SCATTERED PILGRIMS*

We make a living by what we get. We make a life by what we give.

WINSTON CHURCHILL

Meditate on Scripture

Do not be afraid, little flock, for your Father has been pleased to give you the kingdom. Sell your possessions and give to the poor. Provide purses for yourselves that will not wear out, a treasure in heaven that will not be exhausted, where no thief comes near and no moth destroys. For where your treasure is, there your heart will be also. (Luke 12:32-34)

Whoever trusts in his riches will fall,
    but the righteous will thrive like a green leaf. (Proverbs 11:28)

No one can serve two masters. Either he will hate the one and love the other, or he will be devoted to the one and despise the other. You cannot serve both God and Money. (Matthew 6:24)

What I'm trying to do here is to get you to relax, not be so preoccupied with *getting* so you can respond to God's *giving*. People who don't know God and the way he works fuss over these things, but you know both God and how he works. Steep yourself in God-reality, God-initiative, God-provisions. You'll find all your everyday human concerns will be met. Don't be afraid of missing out. You're my dearest friends! The Father wants to give you the very kingdom itself.

Be generous. Give to the poor. Get yourselves a bank that can't go bankrupt, a bank in heaven far from bankrobbers, safe from embezzlers, a bank you can bank on. It's obvious, isn't it? The place where your treasure is, is the place you will most want to be, and end up being. (Luke 12:29-34 *The Message*)

But godliness with contentment is great gain. For we have brought nothing into the world, and we can take nothing out of it. But if we have food and clothing, we will be content with that. People who want to get rich fall into temptation and a trap and into many foolish and harmful desires that plunge men into ruin and destruction. For the love of money is a root of all kinds of evil. Some people, eager for money, have wandered from the faith and pierced themselves with many griefs. (1 Timothy 6:6-10)

Journal Your Thoughts

Where are you with money? What does it mean to you? Jot down your first thoughts about money and its emotional hold over you.

Respond in Prayer

When we bring all of our murky truths about money, safety and faith into the open, they weigh us down until we drop them at our Savior's feet. Let this time of confession free you and lead you into praise and thanksgiving as you find acceptance, forgiveness and love in Christ.

Consider Creation

As you spend time with God, notice how creation is provided for. Where do you need to trust God more for provisions in your life?

Seek Stillness

Let your soul settle. The swirling thoughts about money, God's words: let them all sink into your being. Invite God to bring up what is necessary and important right now. In silence offer God all you have and are and hope to be, and then rest there.

Reflection Questions

What is your earliest memory of money? What messages did your parents give you about finances? How have those early lessons affected your relationship with money and its emotional power in your life?

What do you secretly covet?

Where have you used money—or what it can buy—to feel good about yourself? Consider power, control, safety, acceptance. Where has it supplanted God's love and presence in your life?

What do Jesus' words, "Your heavenly Father gladly gives you the kingdom," mean to you? How might that change the way you live?

How do faith and finances work together in your life? What changes would you like to make in the way you earn, spend, save or give money? What is God leading you to do?

Hymn of Praise

"When I Survey the Wondrous Cross"

When I survey the wondrous cross
On which the Prince of glory died,
My richest gain I count but loss,
And pour contempt on all my pride.

Forbid it Lord, that I should boast,
Save in the death of Christ my God!
All the vain things that charm me most,
I sacrifice them to His blood.

Were the whole realm of nature mine,
That were an offering far too small;
Love so amazing so divine,
Demands my soul, my life, my all.

ISAAC WATTS, 1707

Examen of Conscience

Gently, with Jesus nearby, review your day, your pockets, your purchases. What do your transactions say about your faith? When did you know God's presence and when did you slip away to the world and worry of Mammon? Invite God to bring healing to those soul gaps and help you to rest in Christ's sufficiency.

10 ❧ THE HAPPINESS QUOTIENT

Knowing the Way to Joy

"Happiness isn't scriptural." My friend, a fun and energetic pastor's wife, issued this statement with a very serious face.[3]

Did I hear right? This woman could quote entire books of the Bible, pray for hours through tears and laughter, disciple other women, lead small groups and was a bubbly and sincere wife and friend. But she didn't believe happiness to be scriptural?

Scripture mentions the word *happy* numerous times, and right alongside *happy* is *blessed* as a meaning. That's the preferred interpretation, the word Christians glom onto. That's better, more spiritual than being happy. Sometimes I ask others "How are you?" and wait for a real answer. And sometimes, rather than "fine" these devout believers will answer, "Blessed. I am blessed." Next time, I'm going to ask, "But—are you happy?"

Aren't these byproducts of one another? Surely we are blessed, and so how can we not smile, be happy? And why couldn't happiness be construed as a blessing?

What could be unspiritual about happiness?

---

[3]Portions of this chapter first appeared in "A Happy Spirituality: Back to the Beginning," *Indeed*, March-April 2005, pp. 12-13. Used by permission.

NO HAPPINESS ALLOWED

Christians get very serious about levity. "Life is serious, and then we die," went one mother's axiom for her family. Another friend said, "We never sang 'I've got the joy, joy, joy, joy down in my heart' in my church." As though something must be wrong if we just feel plain happy. How could that be something God doesn't want?

Backtrack to Adam and Eve romping about in Eden, a garden lush and colorful, filled with scent, sound and safety. Were they happy? Happy? They must have felt like exploding with it. Happiness must be one of the first emotions experienced at creation, a primary, pure sensation.

But then, sometimes we have problems with *sensation*. The word is so close to sensual, and then the mind slides to sexual, and pretty soon we have shut down our emotions in fear. *Sensual*—pertaining to our five senses— points to being fully alive, and sensuality can be expressed and experienced in whole and holy ways. *Sensual* doesn't mean "wild and crazy sex outside of marriage." So do we fear being out of control? Sinning because we feel happy?

The pursuit of happiness, happiness as an end in itself, may make us consider this emotion unspiritual. This conjures up images of hedonistic living— self-centered, pleasure-seeking, narcissistic existing, forgetting that a world exists outside of our own gratification.

Illegitimacies may manufacture synthetic happiness. If we believe subconsciously that happiness is derived externally, then we focus on the next thing, substance or person to create happiness. We search relentlessly for the next good feeling. And if that means alcohol or drugs or sex or the rush of winning, well, so what? If happiness is an inalienable right, and we don't experience happiness of our own accord, let the search begin. These excesses we should fear.

But why fear the real thing? The Israelites didn't. The word we translate, simply, as "joy" has sixty-seven different words in Hebrew, sixty-seven nuances of joy. Doesn't sound too sinful, does it? Sounds like a smorgasbord of happiness to me.

Are we just out of practice? Robert grew up with counterfeit happiness.

Alcohol numbed his parents' misery in a difficult marriage. "All I wanted was safety," he said, "I didn't know to look for happiness—I just watched for the vodka. When it came out, I tried to leave." Unhappiness may recreate a familiar childhood feeling and a guardedness against disappointments. Unhappiness can be a habit. And it can be sin.

Maybe we keep our eyes on our list and just try to get through the day, the demands. We don't notice the rainbow or the scent of fall leaves. Snow is a nuisance to be shoveled, scraped and salted rather than a wonderland of snowballs and sled runs. Flowers mean yard work and company means cleaning, and pretty soon we've lost our capacity for fun, for spontaneity. Which is often where happiness appears.

Most behaviors offer some reward or we wouldn't continue them. One benefit to a "happy deficit" is that unhappiness is an attention-getting device. Others ask, "What's wrong?" and we can bask in their negative attention. Unhappiness gives others responsibility for our emotional well-being, so we don't have to change our life approach or step out in faith.

Blame, as well, creates a barrier to happiness.

I'D BE HAPPY IF ONLY . . .

Sean blames his parents for his life's mess: "I'd be happy if they weren't so screwed up." Thelma blames her husband: "If he'd get a job, I'd be happy." Lindsey blames her ex-boyfriend. Blame and happiness are mutually exclusive. In *Happiness Is an Inside Job,* John Powell said, "Growth begins where blaming ends." As does happiness.

Or perhaps we believe that the perfect circumstance will lead to happiness. "I'll be happy if I have money or a girlfriend or a husband or a child or when I get in shape or buy a house or . . ." Maybe making others happy is our job description: If only they are happy, we are happy. We are so busy trying to gauge others' emotional state that we forget to live our own life. The problem with both approaches to living is that no one has that kind of power. Happiness is internal. No one can make us happy. Nor do we have the power to make others happy.

Happiness is a power base. We give away power when we externalize it, seeking it anywhere but from our own attitude and relationship with God. As God increasingly becomes our resting place, as we seek our Shepherd and our happiness derives from a heart full of God rather than circumstances or substances, we move powerfully into the life of the Spirit. Even though it makes no sense whatsoever.

HAPPINESS AS AN OXYMORON

In a world that respins and reinvents and glorifies dysfunction, in a world rife with war, crime, conflict and disaster, is it ridiculous to even talk about happiness, let alone hope for it?

Yes. Of course it is. And it's exactly the upside-down approach Jesus used. "Blessed—happy!—are those who mourn. . . . Blessed—happy!—are the persecuted . . ." (Matthew 5:4, 10, my paraphrase). What sort of insanity is that? Who is happy in light of the world today? All of Jesus' "be happies" are in juxtaposition with cause and effect. Happiness is one big oxymoron according to this man.

Why? Because our focus is not intended to be on fleeting, temporary problems. Our focus is on the King of glory who does reign in spite of seeming evidence to the contrary. All the dissonance and discord stand in sharp contrast to Scripture: we are to "fix our eyes on Jesus" (Hebrews 12:2). The rest of that verse is equally insane: "who for the joy set before him endured the cross, scorning its shame." Christ lived out the oxymoronic state of happiness.

Happiness makes no sense if we read the headlines or listen to the neighbors fight or endure a dateless Friday night; it is lunacy if we believe that these are statements of the final answer. Happiness flies in the face of life in a broken world.

What did Jesus say? "In this world you will have tribulation." Amen, we reply. But Jesus didn't quit there. He said, "Be of good cheer." Oh, right. Now we get to the happiness as denial principle. But wait, he didn't stop there either. "I have overcome the world" (John 16:33, my paraphrase).

Hold on. I want that tattooed on my forehead.

Because I get stuck in the mud—making every grain of dust into a big deal, a mountain—and lose all perspective.

If you can relate, maybe we can devise a joy strategy. If unhappiness is not trusting God, if it's related to fear and if perfect love casts out fear, it leaves lots of room for happiness.

A "BE HAPPY" PLAN

Numerous studies report that happy people tend to be healthier—which makes sense with emotional health the key to overall health.

Perspective. Happiness is a thought away, is determined by the thoughts we embrace and entertain. We are as happy as we choose to think. Friends shared their own motto with me: "You can choose to make this a happy day or a sad day. What will you choose?"

Why choose unhappiness? That's like responding to the offer "You can choose a migraine or a double mocha latte" with "One migraine to go, please." This is not to deny serious issues, such as clinical depression or chronic pain. Our "be happy" plan involves perspective. Will I leave for the day's work saying, "This is going to be an awful day," or "Thank you, God! I'm alive! I will rejoice in another day with you"?

Craig has been unemployed for nearly a year. His wife, Melinda, says, "If I look at two weeks from now, I could freak out. But if I live today, I'm joyful." Annette, diagnosed with cancer and given one year to live, said, "This is the best year of my life. Every moment is precious." By focusing not on her losses, fear or pain, but on each moment as it presented itself, Annette learned a key to happiness: living each moment as if it were indeed her last.

That sounds trite. But perspective is everything. We can mourn with Job, "My eyes will never see happiness again" (Job 7:7), or we can trust that God reigns in spite of worldly evidence. Jesus endured the cross by focusing on coming joy.

Present. Happiness is a choice of how to think at any given moment. Happiness exists only in the present. And by living in the present, by paying attention to a friend's brown eyes or the waggy tail of a dog or the fact that we are breathing, we turn away from the worry or anger or fear or pain territory. Being present can morph into happiness.

Richard Carlson writes, "Regardless of your past experiences, the specifics of your current circumstances, how much you analyze your past or speculate about your future, you will never be happy until you learn to live in the present moment."

Last week, my son and I cheered as temperatures dropped. The windshield wipers began swishing off thickening raindrops. The slush turned to extravagant, wild snowflakes as we drove home. He headed for homework, but soon I called him to survey the scene. "We should go sledding," I said. It was one of my few spur-of-the-moment escapades this past year.

My children seem born for adventure. And yet, even Josh looked at me as though flowers suddenly sprouted from my head, or fireworks. "Now? Right now?" To my yes, he said again, "Are you serious?"

"Absolutely." Out the door we raced, barely stopping for gloves and socks. We roared with laughter when the sled wouldn't budge in the wet snow, and took turns pushing one another down the hill, determined to make a run for the future. Halfway up the hill we stopped for a snowball fight, which turned into a snowman-building contest, then a William Tell simulation as we tried to pitch snowballs at the snowman's top-knot. Soaking wet, filled with life, we tromped inside to hot chocolate, praising God for the surprise snow and the chance to enjoy it. Happy? Is there a stronger word?

We both had pressing projects, endless work. He needed his sleep. I had an early day. But paying attention to the present, we racked up a top-ten favorite memory together.

Presence. Jesus' command—it wasn't a suggestion—to be happy even in the midst of difficulties is totally related to the fact of his presence with us. Henri Nouwen said, "Joy and laughter are the gifts of living in the presence of God and trusting that tomorrow is not worth worrying about." The One who holds our future knows exactly what the future holds, and in his presence we can know the fullness of joy.

I never liked the hymn "Happiness Is to Know the Savior" because the lyrics seemed simplistic, kindergartenish. Yet isn't this bottom-line truth? Life—happiness—isn't about the job or the car or the house or the boyfriend or the incoming mail. Life is about—life is found in—Jesus. Only Jesus. "And he himself is our life." "We are complete in him." "In him we live and move and have our being." So if something is missing in the day, if a smiling heart is the last thing we expect when glancing in the mirror, maybe we are looking in the wrong place, again. And we need to redirect to the presence of Jesus in the midst of the uncertainty of our times and the blaring headlines of our soul.

And if that's the case, then we need to put on our dancin' shoes.

THE HAPPY DANCE

One friend waited a lifetime for the right mate to surprise her in her singleness. When he did, she hesitated to count on happiness, to mark this period in her life with too much exuberance. All her friends were ready to do the happy dance, to celebrate God's goodness.

When is the right time to rejoice? When do we get to dance?

We can't wait to do the happy dance until all the elements in our life are perfect. Not when so many little moments string together and create a garland of happiness, a bridal veil of joy—whether there is an earthly mate at the altar or not.

Friends help us have perspective: "It's okay to dance." Even if the ring doesn't show or the relationship disintegrates. Even if the world crumbles tomorrow into a heap and your hopes along with it. Happiness isn't about security. It is about paying attention, celebrating God's presence in our present. Because our Bridegroom is with us now, we dance. Now.

GIVING HAPPINESS, FINDING HAPPINESS

Albert Schweitzer said, "I don't know what your destiny will be, but one thing I know: the only ones among you who will be really happy are those who will have sought and found how to serve." When we serve others, our feet slide into Jesus' sandals. He who came not to be served but to serve showed us the route to happiness. Finding him, we find meaning and learn to love others with his kind of servant love.

If happiness is knowing we are fulfilling our purpose—giving God glory—we can be happy when using our gifts. Giving of our time, talents, treasures not only breaks the self-centered, centrifugal pull of unhappiness and its pursuit, it also breaks through the barriers erected by pain and problems.

We met Mike when he came to church with only half an arm, a new wife and a sweet stepdaughter. We rejoiced at their son's birth and mourned when cancer returned. But Mike didn't stop. He swallowed his chemotherapy pill on his lunch hour and then went back to work. His constant smile and offers to help transformed others. He built a computer for us, crawling around, running lines, typing with five fingers and one stub. He kept loving right up until the Lord called him home. He lived the life God gave him and called him to live, and he was happy.

A Suspicious Happiness

A vacation, like happiness, is internal rather than external. So when fog delayed and canceled connecting flights in Atlanta, though I was hurrying to get a few days' respite, I chose to consider the long hours as a time to shift from the work rush to a mindset of rest. I mulled over happiness instead of missed flights and delayed getaways. I was one of the few people smiling between Chicago and Daytona Beach. Others probably thought I had escaped from an asylum.

Happy people are suspect, especially in airports logjammed with customers who have missed their flights. As if perhaps happy people don't have all the facts. Or have been sniffing the markers in their briefcase. Or bellying up to the wrong bar.

Happy people must not read the headlines or the flight displays, or else they have a lower IQ than the long-faced, sober, good Christians. Or maybe they are living in the manic phase of bipolar disorder. Nancy said, "My sister was such a happy child. She smiled all the time." She paused. "My mom was afraid she was mentally ill."

THE HAPPY STRETCH

Happy children are children who are loved, kept safe with suitable boundaries and allowed to play. I loved stretching out on the floor beside our toddlers while they played. Happily. Engrossed in their toys or blocks or books or pots and pans. Safe with me nearby, laughing and loving them.

Here's the deal with kids: happy, healthy children laugh one hundred or more times a day. Adults do well to trip the switch fifteen times in twenty-four hours. Maybe Jesus was onto something when he said "Unless you change and become like little children, you will never enter the kingdom of heaven" (Matthew 18:3). The very state of happiness requires trust, and trust is integral to a healthy childhood. Hand in hand, these lead us to heaven.

How do we forget that when we grow up? Somehow I think God would be pleased if we were, you know, happy.

Maybe we don't trust our Shepherd enough. He invites us to stretch out beside still waters, to restore our soul. Listen to that. Restoration, to bring back to its original state.

Hmm. Might that include—happy?

So I'm going to try to sit still long enough to notice where I'm not trusting God. Long enough to discern his presence with me. Long enough to let him restore my soul. And I'll just bet it becomes a restful, restorative process. I bet that if I lay down in green pastures long enough, I will notice God stretched out alongside me, keeping me safe, loving me. And I will laugh. With happiness. Instead of my quiet time, I will call it my "happy hour."

Join me? It's on the house.

FOR YOUR RETREAT

Quotes to Contemplate

God is the Creator and the protector and the lover. For until I am substantially united to him, I can never have perfect rest or true happiness, until, that is, I am so attached to him that there can be no created thing between my God and me.

JULIAN OF NORWICH, *SHOWINGS*

It's so much easier to be happy, my love. It's so much easier to choose to love the things that you have—and you have so much—instead of always yearning for what you're missing or what it is you're imagining you're missing. It's so much more peaceful.

KATE GULDEN, PLAYED BY MERYL STREEP, IN *ONE TRUE THING*

Happiness is a state of mind, not a set of circumstances. It is a serene feeling you can always experience and live in, not something you have to search very far for. In fact, you can never find happiness by "searching," because the moment you do, you imply that it is found outside yourself.

RICHARD CARLSON, *YOU CAN BE HAPPY NO MATTER WHAT*

We thank Thee, Lord, for the glory of the late days and the excellent face of Thy sun. We thank Thee for good news received. We thank Thee for the pleasures we have enjoyed and for those we have been able to confer. And now, when the clouds gather and rain impends over the forest and our house, permit us not to be cast down; let us not lose the savor of past mercies and past pleasures; but, like the voice of a bird singing in the rain, let grateful memory survive in the hour of darkness.

ROBERT LOUIS STEVENSON

To live fully, outwardly and inwardly, not to ignore the external reality for the sake of the inner life, or the reverse—that's quite a task.

ETTY HILLESUM

Everyone will be called to account for all the legitimate pleasures which he or she has failed to enjoy.

THE TALMUD

Happiness that the world cannot take away only flourishes in the secret garden of our souls. By tending to the inner garden and uprooting the weeds of external expectations, we can nurture our authentic happiness the way we would nurture something that's beautiful and alive. Happiness is a living emotion . . . not a frivolous, expendable luxury.

SARAH BAN BREATHNACH, *SIMPLE ABUNDANCE*

Meditate on Scripture

An anxious heart weighs a man down,
   but a kind word cheers him up. (Proverbs 12:25)

Now is your time of grief, but I will see you again and you will rejoice, and no one will take away your joy. . . . Ask and you will receive, and your joy will be complete. . . .

In this world you will have trouble. But take heart! I have overcome the world. (John 16:22, 24, 33)

Praise be to the God and Father of our Lord Jesus Christ! In his great mercy he has given us new birth into a living hope through the resurrection of Jesus Christ from the dead, and into an inheritance that can never perish, spoil or fade—kept in heaven for you. . . . Though you have not seen him, you love him; and even though you do not see him now, you believe in him and are filled with an inexpressible and glorious joy, for you are receiving the goal of your faith, the salvation of your souls. (1 Peter 1:3-4, 8-9)

A happy heart makes the face cheerful,
    but heartache crushes the spirit. (Proverbs 15:13)

Let all who take refuge in you be glad;
    let them ever sing for joy.
Spread your protection over them,
    that those who love your name may rejoice in you.
For surely, O LORD, you bless the righteous;
    you surround them with your favor as with a shield. (Psalm 5:11-12)

May the God of hope fill you with all joy and peace as you trust in him, so that you may overflow with hope by the power of the Holy Spirit. (Romans 15:13)

I have set the LORD always before me.
    Because he is at my right hand,
    I will not be shaken.
Therefore my heart is glad and my tongue rejoices;

my body also will rest secure,
because you will not abandon me to the grave,
nor will you let your Holy One see decay.
You have made known to me the path of life;
you fill me with joy in your presence,
with eternal pleasures at your right hand. (Psalm 16:8-11)

Journal Your Thoughts

What makes you happy? Spend time with that thought, the biases you may have about happiness, the circumstances or people who have dictated your feelings. Where are you now in terms of your HQ (happiness quotient)? What is holding you back from the fullness of joy?

Respond in Prayer

If happiness exists only in the present, then prayer is a perfect place to encounter happiness. Pour all the worries and fears out, and ask Christ to fill you with his presence and peace. This will turn your heart to praise and thanksgiving.

Consider Creation

Maybe a tour of the produce department is in order. Stroll the aisles unencumbered and unhurried. Pick up a package of fresh strawberries. Turn them over and breathe deeply of their red, ripe sweetness. Stay with that sensation and invite God into the midst of it. What do you feel there? Ever wonder why God went to the trouble to make such beautiful goodies that are also perfumed and healthy? Because God loves you more than life itself and longs to see your delighted sniffing of strawberries today, and to have you turn your heart to praise, noticing the gift of the moment.

Seek Stillness

As your heart hushes and settles, be content to just rest here in the arms of the Shepherd.

Reflection Questions

What is your happiest memory? How do you feel about happiness and spirituality, unhappiness and fear and sin? Are you basically happy? What would others say about your happiness quotient?

There are many reasons to feel unhappy. What are some of yours? And where do you prefer to live? Where does blame fit into your happy package?

What is the difference between happiness and denial? How might you live with joy in unresolved problems, pain or difficult relationships?

When has your sense of happiness increased because of serving others? When have you felt torn about helping others in order to feel good about yourself versus serving from your fullness in Christ?

What changes would you need to make in your attitude and heart to experience more happiness?

Hymn of Praise

"O Happy Day, That Fixed My Choice"

O happy day, that fixed my choice

On thee, my Savior and my God
Well may this glowing heart rejoice,
and tell its raptures all abroad.

It's done: the great transaction's done!
I am the Lord's and he is mine;
He drew me and I followed on,
Charmed to confess the voice divine.

Now rest, my long divided heart,
Fixed on this blissful center, rest.
Here have I found a nobler part;
Here heavenly pleasures fill my breast.

Chorus:
Happy day, happy day,
When Jesus washed my sins away
He taught me how to watch and pray,
And live rejoicing every day.
Happy day, happy day,
When Jesus washed my sins away!

PHILIP DODDRIDGE, 1755; REFRAIN FROM WESLEYAN SACRED HARP

Examen of Conscience

Think back on your day. Where did you experience joy? What robbed you of happiness? When did you allow worry over the future or pain from the past to block the sun? Bring that before God. Invite our wacky Savior to bring the bubblings of happiness, and watch for that. Find grace for the places where the joy was stolen. Sweet dreams.

11 ⟡ REAL POWER

Exploring the Key to Strength and Purity

High school. The "power players" huddled on the football field or cheered at the bleachers. I hunkered in the stands with my friends, freezing and wearing a hideous band uniform that looked like a Fourth of July space suit. (Band members are rarely power players, it appears. Unless they play their instruments with vigor.) Cheerleaders bounced and beamed.

The ball snapped. Cheers rose.

A stray puppy wandered onto the track and plopped down in front of a cheerleader. Looking annoyed, she kicked the puppy out of her way. The crowd booed. Realizing her strategic mistake, she tried to reinstate her image by petting the dog.

This memory hurts me; I see the puppy cringe and sense the wounding that comes from loving and trusting another, and then being kicked in response. Sometimes I have been the puppy. But more often, I have been the kicker, abusing my power by hurting others.

Power is not something we associate with personal retreats or even with Christianity. Power goes against our notions of humility. And many people see power used to harm—harm them, harm those they love.

In this time with our Shepherd, as we choose to abandon the power of pushing forward in our daily life, we seek the power that comes from laying down our lists and agendas, bringing our needs to our Savior. When we find him as our resting place, power is restored: power that heals, helps, and brings Christ's love and hope to a dying world.

POWERFUL POSSIBILITIES

I close my eyes, feeling my impotence. Feeling the pain of my inability to live this life well. Knowing that I have walked away from God's presence day after day and have hurt others in my attempts to manage my own life in my sinful, self-oriented, fear-based, task-driven focus. Knowing that when the time comes to love, I too often fold and run.

What does it take to live a life in the presence and the power of the risen Christ? To experience the miracle might of the Most High?

I have no easy answers. But the One who broke the power of death and the death sentence of sin by his own death on a cross, the One who burst free from the bonds of the enemy and rose to triumphant new life, this One, who clung to the power of God throughout his entire earthly life that he might be a sinless offering, this One waits, now, offering us the same power. The power to cling.

But this is not the power we have come to expect in life.

POWER POINTS

We live in a world that buys into power in all possible forms, and we are not exempt from the allure. Power images assault us.

It may look like money with its purchasing power for respect, status symbols, trophy spouses, television shows and political favor. Maybe power comes from the back room—or the bush. In the *Survivor* segment I observed on TV, participants' value came from their perseverance. And "backroom" deal-making. They schemed to convince others of their leadership ability, to inveigle trust and to collude to vote a member off the island. Too often, power works for one person's interest only: the winner's.

Makeover shows proclaim: I have the power to change your life! Whether it's a house or a spouse or a face or a child. One program showed women prematurely aged, missing teeth, poorly dressed and with bad hair. After visits to plastic and oral surgeons, celebrity makeup artists, hair designers and a department store, the pictures before and after bore faint resemblance to one another.

But wouldn't real power change more than the external? If life circumstances don't change, if the ambushed people do not have the heart or wisdom to live in their new faces well, how long will the external last? Not long in bodies designed for planned obsolescence.

Beauty is a power card. Heads turn, dates line up, you get to audition for bachelor or bachelorette "reality" shows (as though that is anyone's true reality). Yet beautiful people rarely feel beautiful, and our bodies' natural downward slide through aging creates great anxiety for many—and great expense as they try to renovate and repair the depreciation and damage. Beauty becomes its own curse as people either idolize you or steer clear of you in fear. Beauty may include inherent loneliness, if you can't believe anyone loves you with pure motives.

Some power players in our world today made a fortune with their brains. These may not have been the popular people in high school, but when the real world starts counting, brain power wins big points, especially when accompanied by loads of money and at least fame, some big-selling patents or brand recognition.

Sin may create a sense of power, of "I'm above the rules." For instance, when we who are forgiven refuse to forgive, we wield power—sinfully. Paul asked, "You who preach against stealing, do you steal? You who say that people should not commit adultery, do you commit adultery?" (Romans 2:21-22). The abuse of power creates a subtle soul deterioration.

Unfortunately, whether it looks like sports, beauty, sex, money, brains, sin or even passivity or codependency, we all make a stab for power. We spend much of our lives vying for a power position.

POWER, PROFILE, PROBLEMS

Power commandeers headlines daily. A recent front page featured a man winning the lottery, a social worker murdered in a foreign country and a story about someone killed in a rollover crash. Abused, power becomes self-centered and breeds control over others. Like the abuser who harms a weaker person or the rapper whose violent lyrics generate a following and a resplendent lifestyle, young people decide that imitation is the sincerest form of flattery. They are harmed, and they harm others. Without morals, power corrupts.

People become manipulative, trying to wheedle favor or trickle-down power benefits, taking advantage of others in power. Ask your state lottery winners how many people and groups appeared for handouts when their winning tickets were pulled, and how much the power of money changed their lives for the better.

There must be more to power than this. For people who love Christ, power must assume a different form and look different than it looks to the rest of the world.

THE JESUS JUXTAPOSITIONS

Power through compassion rarely makes the front page. We don't equate power with serving others. It's one more Jesus juxtaposition—where opposites reside alongside one another and somehow make sense.

Jesus was full of this type of contradiction. He constantly confounded the world's definitions, turned religion into a real relationship with God rather than a bunch of rules. Jesus came on the scene in power—healing, casting out demons, raising people from the dead, shushing the storm and feeding thousands from some bread crusts. But he didn't raise a fist to his attackers, didn't answer his accusers, didn't turn away from the poor or the prostitute or the politician. Jesus' power came from serving, from seeing people's desperate need, from an inner silence where he plugged into God and listened and leaned.

Jesus' power showed a solid sterling quality: a purity and love that reflected God. And people whose power base resulted from oppression or abuse or money or judicial reign violently hated him for it.

If you grew up with "Gentle Jesus meek and mild," then equating Jesus with power may not come naturally. But without doubt the most powerful man who ever lived, Jesus' power brought with it humility and dependency on the power and presence and promise of God within him. This Jesus declared that power comes from death: Christ's death grants us life. What an example of the upside-down nature of the gospel, where the King of the universe is born in a cave to impoverished parents, where the conquering hero rides in on a donkey instead of a stallion, where the Messiah kneels and washes his disciples' feet, and where victory looks like death on a cross.

POWER FOR THE PEOPLE

Scripture resounds with examples of God's power to redeem, restore, create, ransom from the grave, deliver from evil, forgive, save, and defeat death, to name a few. Christ's word was "with power" (Luke 4:32 KJV). Other verses speak of the power God gives us: to heal, to make disciples, to use our gifts, to labor in God's power that works mightily within us (Ephesians 3:20).

God's power fills the Bible, and the power God confers on us comes by virtue of our "Yes!" to Christ. But if we don't live in the *power* or the *love* of Christ, well, heaven's nice, but what about *this* life? Paul did say, after all, "I can do all things through Christ who strengthens me" (Philippians 4:13).

This is unfortunately not my reality much of the time. While wrestling with my own spiritual impotence and the meaning of power in my life, I realized that I have to choose to let go of my safety mechanisms in order to truly experience God's power within me.

Power comes when I learn to abandon my agenda. It's that choice again: where do I want to live? Jesus said, "Abide in me." He also said, "By myself I can do nothing" (John 5:30). "Anyone who has faith in me will do what I have been doing. He will do even greater things than these" (John 14:12), but we can do nothing apart from him. Nothing. Nothing. Nothing. Nothing that lasts.

Christ is not seeking robots to plug into the outlet and set on automatic pilot. He wants people who will love him enough, trust him enough, long for him enough that they will let go of their own control, abandon their abandonment reflexes, relinquish their anger. He wants people to choose him, to believe he has a better plan.

Obedience can't be separated from power. Power can't be separated from surrender.

So does this look like a rush of filling, a gush of strength, a wave of righteousness?

No, probably not. It looks like recognizing the battle both within and without and turning to the Savior with the chaos that comes from struggling. It looks like an interior conversation that moves us into the presence of Christ again.

It looks like reaching out, though tired and empty, with a prayer for God's filling. Like initiating time with another when we'd rather hole up alone. Like an act of love in a busy day.

It looks like taking a call from someone who will need time and attention and possibly lots of it, when you'd rather let voice mail take over. It looks like a "Help, God!" prayer breathed on the run. And seamlessly the transition begins to be made from our power to God's.

This doesn't seem superhuman or glamorous or particularly remarkable. Didn't Jesus say, "You'll do greater works than I'm doing"? But we can't possibly estimate the impact of one life, lived under the power of the Holy Spirit, as that life intersects with others who are gasping for a breath of the Savior.

THE FORM OF GODLINESS AND THE POWER

In a final scene in *The Phantom of the Opera*, Raoul posed on a high banister, then executed a perfect swan dive into the waters of the catacombs to rescue his beloved Christine. Was it a real dive? Yes, he had to get into the right form. He had to propel himself off the banister. But the audience couldn't see the grappling hook and line connecting him securely to the catwalk. Without that line and hook, Raoul would have smacked the "water," breaking all the bones in his body. He'd be dead, Christine wouldn't have been rescued and would have married the Phantom.

Our grappling hook, our line, is the connection with the Holy Spirit. The more we develop the obedience habit from a praying center—doing the right thing even when we don't feel like it or are afraid—the more we will be aware of the possibilities of living in God's power. The more we lay down our rights and desires and grievances in order to align our heart with God's heart, the quicker our ability to access God's presence and to hear that still small voice urging us to act or speak or love.

We practice our form: arms spread, knees slightly bent. And then we make sure the hook is attached to us and to the line, and we dive.

And God's power holds us, carries us.

A POWER PLAN

In December 2004 a deadly tsunami jarred the Indian Ocean with a force that registered around the world. A warning system to alert officials of the catastrophic power looming under the sea might have spared thousands of lives, but the system was turned off. Just so, many Christians have been wrecked when their power failed in a clutch. A commitment to integrity is not enough. The Scriptures warn us that "people will be lovers of themselves, lovers of money, boastful, proud, abusive, disobedient to their parents, ungrateful, unholy, without love, unforgiving, slanderous, without self-control, brutal, not lovers of the good, . . . [not] lovers of God—having a form of godliness but denying its power" (2 Timothy 3:2-5).

We need a warning system. Following are some components of a power plan for personal growth and for emergencies.

Prayer. Prayer, both alone and with others, puts us in the presence of God, the God of all power, and shifts our center from our own temptations, weaknesses or struggles to God's ability. In prayer we fill up our empty tank with God.

Purpose. A life purpose works for eternal, not just external, change or earthly control. This focuses us on the right kind of power.

Repentance. Never underestimate the power of a repentant heart in breaking down defensiveness and opening others to the power of God.

Presence. Brother Lawrence had it right. Power comes from practicing God's presence, from a steady turning to God throughout our days and a filling with God's Word.

Purity and accountability. Have an emergency number when temptation rises. One man, addicted to pornography, installed safety software on his computers to alert himself and an accountability partner if he tried to access pornographic sites. He had safeguards and a realistic understanding of his own fallibility. He also met weekly with a support group and his account-ability friend.

A SHEPHERD'S POWER

Power comes not from the wad of bills in your pocket or the car you drive, not from your GPA or your home run record, not from your ability to wran-gle the best contract or sell the most widgets or raise the most gifted or obe-dient children.

Real power comes from laying down our life. From relinquishing our own grasps at power. When we cease striving, we will know the ultimate power: God.

Power comes
Not from taking up arms
   But from laying down our lives.
Not from worry and work
   But from worship.
Not from seizing
   But from serving.
Not from grasping
   But from giving.
Not from being right
   But from being repentant.
Not from my will
   But from God's.
Not from self-sufficiency
   But from surrender to the Shepherd.
Power comes
   From being loved.

For Your Retreat

Quotes to Contemplate

You want so much to heal yourself, fight your temptations, and stay in control. But you cannot do it yourself. . . . You have to say yes fully to your powerlessness in order to let God heal you. Your willingness to experience your powerlessness already includes the beginning of surrender to God's acting in you, . . . your willingness to let go of your desire to control your life reveals a certain trust. The more you relinquish your stubborn need to maintain power, the more you get in touch with the One who has the power to heal and guide you. And the more you get in touch with that divine power, the easier it will be to confess to yourself and to others your basic powerlessness.

HENRI J. M. NOUWEN, *THE INNER VOICE OF LOVE*

> *Lord, I am overwhelmed at the wonder that when*
> *You came to live in me,*
> *You brought Your love to live in me.*
> *You enable me to do—and to be—*
> *more than I ever could on my own.*
> *So live Your life through me,*

extend Your grace through me,
heal and bless through me,
serve and encourage through me,
and love others extravagantly through me.
I can do all these things—because Your love
continually empowers me!
Amen

NANCY STAFFORD,
THE WONDER OF HIS LOVE

I believe the Lord helps those
who set out to do great things for his sake
and never fails those who trust in him alone,
who depend on him to meet all their needs.
This does not mean
that I am excused from seeking to help myself,
only that in trusting him I will be free from anxiety.
I prefer to have around me
People who help me to believe that this is so.
I try to surround myself
with people who seem to be making progress
in the love and service of God,
with those who place their trust in God alone.
I seek out those who are
single-minded and courageous
in their desire to do great things for the Lord,
and who place all their trust in him.

TERESA OF ÁVILA,
LET NOTHING DISTURB YOU

Meditate on Scripture

I want to know Christ and the power of his resurrection and the fellowship of sharing in his sufferings, becoming like him in his death, and so, somehow, to attain to the resurrection of the dead. . . .

Our citizenship is in heaven. And we eagerly await a Savior from there, the Lord Jesus Christ, who, by the power that enables him to bring everything under his control, will transform our lowly bodies so that they will be like his glorious body. (Philippians 3:10-11, 20-21)

But you will receive power when the Holy Spirit comes on you; and you will be my witnesses in Jerusalem, and in all Judea and Samaria, and to the ends of the earth. (Acts 1:8)

[Jesus said,] "The man who loves his life will lose it, while the man who hates his life in this world will keep it for eternal life. Whoever serves me must follow me; and where I am, my servant also will be. My Father will honor the one who serves me." (John 12:25-26)

You, my brothers, were called to be free. But do not use your freedom to indulge the sinful nature; rather, serve one another in love. (Galatians 5:13)

Therefore, . . . in view of God's mercy, . . . offer your bodies as living sacrifices, holy and pleasing to God—this is your spiritual act of worship. Do not conform any longer to the pattern of this world, but be transformed by the renewing of your mind. Then you will be able to test and approve what God's will is—his good, pleasing and perfect will. (Romans 12:1-2)

But [the Lord] said to me, "My grace is sufficient for you, for my power is made perfect in weakness." Therefore I will boast all the more gladly about my weaknesses, so that Christ's power may rest on me. That is why, for Christ's sake, I delight in weaknesses, in insults, in hardships, in persecutions, in difficulties. For when I am weak, then I am strong. (2 Corinthians 12:9-10)

Now to him who is able to do immeasurably more than all we ask or imagine, according to his power that is at work within us, to him be glory in the church and in Christ Jesus throughout all generations, for ever and ever! Amen. (Ephesians 3:20-21)

For God did not give us a spirit of timidity, but of power, of love and of self-discipline. (2 Timothy 1:7)

Journal Your Thoughts

Invite God to show you where a hunger for power consumes you, where power is or has been wielded inappropriately in your life. Spend time journaling about power that harmed you.

Respond in Prayer

Consider Psalm 68:18, 32-35 as you move in praise to God. Ask the Holy Spirit to open your eyes to the places where you have done God's work in your power, where you have backed away from the next right action or word because of old safety mechanisms—don't trust, feel, love or serve because you might get hurt. Bring these broken places to God, asking for forgiveness, healing and the ability to trust the Holy Spirit's power in you.

Consider Creation

Where do you witness God's power in creation? How does this affect you? If God is powerful, reigning over all the earth, what implications does this have for you? Your daily life? Your biggest problem? As you spend time in creation today, ask God to speak into your soul power that comes from knowing the King of all the earth.

Seek Stillness

Let God's Word fill you. Then, silence your heart and intersect with the most powerful being in the universe. Quietly cease striving and struggling; surrender your agenda, demands and problems. Spend time loving God without needing a response or good feeling from the time.

Reflection Questions

How would you define power? How did your family of origin use, abuse or refuse power? What power tools do you rely on?

Name the most powerful event of your life. How did this affect you? Those you love?

When do you feel helpless? When do you try to take power into your own hands? When does your power hurt others? When do you most long for God's power to be displayed in your life? What would that look like?

When have you seen God's power revealed? When have you known God's power working through you? When have God's power and might accomplished what you could not?

When do you think you need a power plan? Describe your personal power plan.

Hymn of Praise

"Come, Thou Almighty King"

Come, thou almighty King,
Help us Thy Name to sing, help us to praise!
Father all glorious, o'er all victorious,
Come and reign over us, Ancient of Days!

Come, Thou incarnate Word,
Gird on thy mighty sword, our prayer attend!
Come, and Thy people bless, and give Thy Word success;
Spirit of holiness, On us descend!

Come, holy Comforter,
Thy sacred witness bear in this glad hour.
Thou Who almighty art, now rule in every heart,
And ne'er from us depart, Spirit of power!

ANONYMOUS (SOME SOURCES CREDIT CHARLES WESLEY, 1757)

Examen of Conscience

Go gently back through your day with the Shepherd. Where in the day did you try to work in your power? Where were God's presence and power manifest? Invite God to heal the ravages in your soul from being in a broken world.

12 ❧ CRAZY ABOUT YOU

Discovering You Are God's Beloved

"What is your greatest fear?" the pastor asked. The people shared their answer with their pew neighbors. The gorgeous twenty-year-old near me said, "That I will never find a husband who will love me." If this young woman, who is also bright, witty and compassionate, was worried about finding the love of her life, what hope is there for the Plain Janes and Ordinary Joes of this world?

WRINKLES IN TIME

Hollywood, romance novels and the Internet provide strong images of the "great lover." There is, of course, one wrinkle in this fantasy: the celluloid models portraying the ideal lover are in reality human beings. Even these well-chiseled or shapely people may have stand-ins for skin scenes. They have flaws. And flaws are what we do not want in our dream image. Trusting someone with flaws, someone who sins, someone who leaves dishes in the sink or socks on the floor or the car with an empty gas tank—trusting someone with even minor faults means getting hurt. Who wants to stand in line for the perfect lover only to get hurt?

Once, in a rough spot in our marriage, I faced my glaring imperfections and feelings of worthlessness, and eventually realized as well that this man I married, handsome and wonderful and filled with the love of Christ, also somehow fell short of the mark. We ran into our own and one another's woundedness and failings.

DISAPPOINTED IN LOVE

We have all been jilted and are in some way jaded and jaundiced. We have been loved imperfectly. We have been damaged by trusting someone who turned out to be fallible. We have expected heaven and gotten earth. A parent betrayed or abandoned us, or a date stood us up, or someone took advantage of us, or a feckless steady broke our heart or used us and dropped us. A part of our heart is stubborn and stonelike and unwilling to trust again.

Our fears zoom into focus: we are not good enough. We are not lovable. We are not worthy. No one can treat us with the love and respect we so crave. Not that we deserve that love, anyway.

No one, that is, this side of the movies or this side of a page-turning romance with a buff man and a full-breasted beauty on the front. Or this side of heaven.

DESTINED FOR FAILURE

Perhaps our love affairs on earth are destined for failure; that is part of the plan. If we found the perfect suitor, the ideal lover, the companion who would read our minds, never leave us, never hurt us, delight always in us no matter whether we get cellulose in our rear from too much sitting or a spare tire from too much indulging—if we found this perfect specimen we would honestly believe that our needs and intense cravings could be satiated on earth.

Whatever our age—college coed or suave single or married with children or retired grandpa—God designed life so that our deepest longings would never be fulfilled by another human being. The Bridegroom created us for heaven and for his own heart.

This Lover is beyond any earthly, earth-bound images. When we run out of the fog and reach the end of our nightmare, the Bridegroom still waits for us. God never abandons us with our wandering eye and faithless, fear-filled heart. This Lover reads our minds and waits with the perfect words, the exact actions, all that we need to be deeply loved.

LOOK NO FURTHER FOR THE PERFECT LOVER

In college and early in careers, friends and I created lists of the perfect husband; bulleted items included everything from looks and height to spiritual depth to intellect to humor to physical fitness and a call to ministry. But in our inexperience and naiveté we missed many qualities. We didn't think about a lover who would love us even when we sin and our bodies sag or our faces wrinkle and our tan lines fade. We didn't think about a no-matter-what lover.

Reading David's words about God in Psalm 139 move me immensely as I read them with the longings of a lover. These verses include attributes we desperately seek in an earth mate. Where else would we ever find this kind of love? This Lover

- loves us even though knowing us thoroughly (v. 1)
- anticipates all our moves (v. 2)
- figures out our actions in spite of our messy and poor communication skills (v. 3)
- reads our lips before words even form (v. 4)
- surrounds us with love and touches us (v. 5)
- is beyond our wildest imaginings (v. 6)
- will never avoid or evade us (v. 7)
- follows us to the ends of the earth (vv. 8-9)
- guides us and holds us fast (v. 10)
- shows up with a nightlight (vv. 11-12)
- designed us and thinks we are wonderful, beautiful (vv. 13-14)
- sees us as we are and as we will be, and loves us anyway (vv. 15-16)
- has a daily route and plan for our life travels (v. 16)
- thinks of us all the time, more than the grains of sand (vv. 17-18)
- and we aren't even dreaming—this is the real deal (v. 18)

- protects us (vv. 19-22)
- wants to receive our anxieties and ugliness (v. 23)
- always leads us into life and destines us for holiness (v. 24)

We can put away the want ads. We've found the perfect match.

If you have never experienced a love relationship like Jesus offers, this is the right time! If you know that you have blown it, that you have sinned, tell that to Jesus. Invite Jesus to come, be the Love of your life, save you from your sin and take you to heaven one day. He promises that if we receive him, we become children of God (John 1:12), that the seal of the Holy Spirit is our wedding band (2 Corinthians 1:22; Ephesians 1:13), and that he will never leave us (Hebrews 13:5). If you pray, inviting Christ to come and live in you, to be your Lover and your Savior, tell someone else, and then start getting to know the Lover of your soul by reading and studying the Bible, being still with him and loving him. And get ready for the greatest adventure of your life.

But just as the sirens sing to turn us away from our earthly mate, so they will tempt us, trying to lure us away from the Lover of our soul. Words will traipse across our mind: "God doesn't love you. You aren't good enough. Head to the fridge, ice cream helps. This isn't real—you need to work harder, give more, practice self-flagellation." These are the sirens calling us, the enemy's voice trying to shut out and out shout the truth: God loves us no matter what, and Jesus said, "No one can snatch you from my hand" (John 10:28, my paraphrase).

A LOVE THAT CHANGES LIVES

When Rich and I got engaged, we both felt that we would be more effective in God's kingdom together than separately. We wanted our love to do more than feel good to us—we wanted it to make a difference in the lives of others around us. What I didn't realize was that by marrying him, I would become a truer person. That our relationship would bring out the best in me. (And in the process cause me to run into the worst in me!)

The same is true of our love affair with God. This love is too good to keep! And it is such a radical love that we cannot remain unchanged. Incredible love changes our heart, changes the way we interact with others, changes our actions and ingrained habits and leads us into health and holiness. This is a love that, once truly experienced, changes the world. John told us, "You will know us by our loving" (1 John 5:2, my paraphrase). This is not an intellectual relationship, a matter of mere mind games, this is truly an *affaire du coeur.*

Does that bother you or feel like a stretch? That God intended all along that we would both know his love and feel his love? We know that faith is not about feelings, but Scripture speaks too loudly to ignore. David says this Lover leads us beside still waters, restores our souls, feeds us a banquet in the desert; lets us live with him forever. This doesn't sound theoretical to me. And Jesus said we must love the Lord our God with all our heart, all our soul, all our mind and all our strength, and love our neighbor as ourself (Mark 12:30-31). He did not omit heart, as we are tempted to do.

This is a love that changes us *and* changes others by the way we are enabled to love.

WHEN YOU'VE "LOST YOUR FIRST LOVE": RENEWING OUR LOVE

Marriage manuals speak of the little things marrieds can do to spice up their lives. After the honeymoon stage, even the greatest romance may lose some of its luster and storybook quality. Real life invades the dream, the clean-the-house, pay-the-bills, work-through-issues type of life that tarnishes the wedding silver and dims the lights. And other substitutes sneak into the resulting disappointment: we spend more time at work or on the phone or pursuing hobbies or cruising the Internet, or we dabble in liaisons that seem exciting but will ultimately destroy our heart and our love relationship.

Jesus said to the church in Ephesus, "You have forsaken your first love. . . . Repent and do the things you did at first" (Revelation 2:4-5). In a courtship, with the brilliant bloom of fresh, new love, what did we do? Rich rode his bicycle 150 miles in a single day through southern Indiana to see me, appearing at the bank where I worked with a cup of steaming coffee, complete with cream. When he left for his night job, he would find notes from me on his steering wheel or chocolates on the dash. On our first anniversary he heard me shut the door on my way in from work and waited at the top of the stairs with his trumpet, playing "Here Comes the Bride." He left on a trip when I was pregnant with our first child, only to ring the doorbell ten minutes later with a bouquet of flowers and the little-boy grin I love plastered on his face.

We did silly things too. Someone gave us a stuffed pickle and put a cape on the green crusader, and that pickle showed up in crazy places. In the medicine cabinet, the microwave, sticking out of a work boot. We left tokens of remembrance in each other's shoes: a penny or a grape or an M&M.

Little acts create a pattern of remembering and renewal, and say, "I thought about you. I love you." These gestures don't have to be complicated and elaborate to shine the silver of our love relationship.

REALISTIC EXPECTATIONS

We make this love affair with God so complex with our expectations of God and of ourselves and what a good romance looks like. If God doesn't behave in a certain way, if Jesus doesn't fit himself into our specific picture of a perfect Lover, then maybe he isn't as good as we thought. We forget that this Lover has foresight and sees the end from the beginning, and knows exactly what we need and when.

And the expectations we haul around of ourselves: A good quiet time should happen every morning for two hours. We need our daily tools: a twenty-pound concordance, a hefty Bible dictionary, a Bible with thousands of study notes, a commentary and reams of paper to record all the brilliant insights about God—after, of course, we have memorized and outlined the entire book of the Bible, and come up with a thesis statement for each chapter and a key verse. We need to read, study, memorize, pray for hours for the needs of the world and preferably on our knees while fasting.

Don't get me wrong. We must have times of deep study in Scripture. Hiding

God's Word in our heart is vital if we are to survive in tough times (i.e., most days). Knowing what the Scripture really means rather than making it fit our lives as we would prefer keeps us living in integrity. Prayer means we take time to listen to God's heart, and let God hear our own. Fasting is one of the best ways to get in touch with our own hunger for God's undying, unbridled love and affection and to offer our hunger pains as a significant sacrifice to God.

These are excellent tools.

But tools cannot, must not, substitute for letting God have our heart. For truly experiencing God's loving presence, God's joy in us. Maybe we need to revamp some of our expectations of courtship.

MINIDATES AND MAGIC MOMENTS

Maybe *reality* is to move back to those little acts of love. Perhaps this looks like breathing deeply, consciously inviting Christ to fill your lungs with his presence. Or like a verse you write out and stuff in your pocket, and every time you reach in for keys or coins or that candy you hid there, you find that verse, and God's Word reminds you that God is the One for you. Or talking out loud to Christ throughout the day.

Carrying a phrase from Scripture on our lips, such as "My grace is sufficient for you" (2 Corinthians 12:9) or "I have loved you with an everlasting love" (Jeremiah 31:3), reminds us of God's very present and practical love, even when other voices howl that we are worthless or undeserving or soon-to-be-abandoned.

Maybe a minidate looks like thirty seconds of stillness, of intense focus and adoration. Or a thank you when we see a love gift—the surprise flowers that bloomed randomly on the deck in the abandoned flower pot. Or the perfect timing of a parking spot. Or a call at just the right moment. One December day I looked up from my work and saw one of God's gifts to me: a swan on the lake. I smiled. Then I looked again. Not one swan—seven swans. Seven swans-a-swimming! And seven days before Christmas. I can only imagine Christ's smile as I glimpsed his present and turned to him. It's all about noticing our Lover and meeting his eyes.

I'M JUST LOVING YOU

Rich and I snuck away for our anniversary, two nights at a house normally used for camp and youth events but recently refurbished. Rich and I work out of our home, when we are home at all, and work often overflows all the margins of our lives and at times ministry swallows our marriage. We seldom leave work, and when we leave the house we bring our work with us as we drive to more ministry work, usually in separate cars.

This house with its thirty-two beds overlooks a large lake outlining a resort community. This November day, temperatures dropped and we battled our way along a path for a couple of hours, fighting stiff winds. By nightfall, the waters were crisping up on the edges in lacy ice. Snow started fluffing about by morning. Icicles hung from twigs and the whole earth shouted "Glory!"

Inside after another windy walk, we built a roaring fire and made good strong coffee. I gathered my favorite supplies (chocolate, a meaty book, my Bible and journal) and snuggled into the sofa near the fireplace. Ten feet away, Rich strummed his guitar.

Work and family matters recessed to the back reaches of my brain, and I noticed my beloved. Appreciation filled me: for his gifts, his integrity, his faith, his love. Looking over my book, I smiled.

He glanced up from plucking the strings, surprised. "What?" he asked. Suspicion curled around the word.

"Nothing. I'm just smiling at you."

"Oh." He went back to his chords. I kept smiling, watching.

Rich looked up again. "What?" His eyes narrowed. "Are you laughing at me?"

"No, Hon. I'm just loving you." Rich's face relaxed, and he smiled broadly in return.

This is our code now. When I'm in Texas or the grocery store and my cell phone lights up with his number, I switch on the phone and say, "I'm smiling at you." I call him when he's on the road and he answers with "I'm smiling at you."

Isn't this a picture of God? God is there, right beside us, and we are busy trying to earn our keep and curry favor and please the world and solve the national debt—or at least our personal version of it. Still, Jesus waits, and when we finally lift our face from our worries, we see those eyes. They beam with love and appreciation and a forever commitment. Jesus just waits to meet our eyes and pour into us his eternal affection.

Do you see him? Can you find his gaze? Do you see that brilliant smile break over his face—like the sunrise—and know: you are his, and he is crazy about you?

And he is . . . just loving you.

And there is no need to look anywhere else. Heaven has come to earth, and you have a Lover who is dying to be with you.

FOR YOUR RETREAT

Quotes to Contemplate

We grow in love of God as we grow in any intimate love relationship—through a continuum of knowing, trusting, desiring, surrendering our defenses and fears, and ultimately our very selves, to the Beloved. That continuum corresponds with the deepening levels of prayer which are encompassed in the process of [reading Scripture: called lectio divina] with its four progressive phases, flowing from reflection on the word of scripture to spontaneous prayer and then to a silent presence to God in love.

RICHARD PEACE, *CONTEMPLATIVE BIBLE READING*

What we are speaking about, in essence, is "falling in love." It is the inescapable message of Jesus' life and teaching that the only real self-fulfillment of life is in giving it away, in love. And it is through the intimate knowledge of his life and love, learned experientially in prayer, that we begin to fathom that "love is his meaning."

THELMA HALL, *TOO DEEP FOR WORDS*

You have loved us first, O God, alas! We speak of it in terms of history as if You have only loved us first but a single time, rather then that without ceasing You have loved us first many times and every day and our whole life through. When we wake up in the morning and turn our soul toward

*you—You are the first—you have loved us first; if I rise at dawn and at
the same second turn my soul toward you in prayer, you are there ahead
of me. You have loved me first.*

SØREN KIERKEGAARD, THE PRAYERS OF KIERKEGAARD

*"Jesus loves me." What would happen if I really believed this? How would
I be different? What would happen if I woke up every morning with the
thought I am loved? What if I moved through my day, ate my lunch, wrote
my articles, read the paper, cooked dinner, with the thought I am loved
always in the front of my mind? How would I respond to my children, greet
my neighbors, treat my fellow employees, negotiate with the auto
mechanic, if I truly lived with a sense of God's love and delight?*

RUTH SENTER, LONGING FOR LOVE

Meditate on Scripture

As a bridegroom rejoices over his bride,
   so will your God rejoice over you. (Isaiah 62:5)

Watch what God does, and then you do it, like children who learn
proper behavior from their parents. Mostly what God does is love you.
Keep company with him and learn a life of love. Observe how Christ
loved us. His love was not cautious but extravagant. He didn't love in
order to get something from us but to give everything of himself to us.
Love like that. (Ephesians 5:1-2 *The Message*)

The LORD your God is with you,
   he is mighty to save.
He will take great delight in you,
   he will quiet you with his love,
      he will rejoice over you with singing. (Zephaniah 3:17)

"In that day," declares the LORD,
  "you will call me 'my husband';
  you will no longer call me 'my master.' . . .
I will betroth you to me forever;
  I will betroth you in righteousness and justice,
  in love and compassion.
I will betroth you in faithfulness,
  and you will acknowledge the LORD." (Hosea 2:16, 19-20)

"Do not be afraid; you will not suffer shame.
  Do not fear disgrace; you will not be humiliated.
You will forget the shame of your youth
  And remember no more the reproach of your widowhood.
For your Maker is your husband—
  the LORD Almighty is his name—
the Holy One of Israel is your Redeemer;
  he is called the God of all the earth.
The LORD will call you back
  as if you were a wife deserted and distressed in spirit—
a wife who married young,
  only to be rejected," says your God. . . .
"[W]ith everlasting kindness
  I will have compassion on you,"
  says the LORD your Redeemer. (Isaiah 54:4-6, 8)

Journal Your Thoughts

Write about your longings for a real, abiding steadfast, unending love. In the safety of your journal listen to your heart before God.

Respond in Prayer

This Lover already knows the worst things about you and will never abandon you. It is safe to share those "worsts" with God, to confess and find grace, to praise and thank God for the gift of never-leaving love.

Consider Creation

The outside world pulsates with God's presence and God's presents to us. The tree, the stream, the brilliant sunrise—all these are a lover's gift, a love note addressed to us. What in nature speaks strongly to you of God's steadfast love for you?

Seek Stillness

Silence is the ultimate gift in paying attention: deep, listening silence, when nothing is more important than being with the beloved. The miracle of miracles: God feels this way about us! Let God's love fill you in the silence as you offer your heart. When thoughts interfere, bring your soul gently back to God's presence.

Reflection Questions

What does your "perfect lover" list of qualifications look like? What images of perfection prejudice your list? When have you been disappointed in love?

When does your relationship with God feel like a love affair? When does it feel like a list of projects to tackle and tools to work through?

How have you sensed God loving you? In what ways do you best experience God's love?

How has God's love changed you? your relationships with others?

What is the deepest longing of your heart regarding the love of your life? If God sings a love song over you, what are the words? What would the song be called?

Hymn of Praise

"O the Deep, Deep Love of Jesus"

O the deep, deep love of Jesus,
Vast, unmeasured, boundless, free!
Rolling as a mighty ocean
In its fullness over me!
Underneath me, all around me,
Is the current of Thy love;
Leading onward, leading homeward,
To my glorious rest above.

O the deep, deep love of Jesus,
Spread His praise from shore to shore!
How He loveth, ever loveth,
Changeth never, nevermore!
How He watches o'er His loved ones,
Died to call them all His own;
How for them He intercedeth,
Watcheth o'er them from the throne.

SAMUEL TREVOR FRANCIS, 1875

Examen of Conscience

Hold your Lover's hand as you go back through your day. Where did you let go of his hand? What happened inside? What were you hoping for? Where did you sense God's love? and communicate that to others? Wait in this place now, inviting God's love and presence to fill you and bring you rest.

Epilogue

En route to the next engagement. My entire body sags into the contours of the window seat and weariness overcomes me. Four hours' sleep last night—business, family, packing. Breathing deeply, I close my sand-blasted eyes. Prayer comes automatically; exhaustion and impossibilities do that.

Oh God. I am too tired to love people. Too tired to complete your work this weekend. Too tired to talk to anyone on this flight. I so need your strength, your compassion. My monologue trails off, and sleep wins. I awaken fifteen minutes later to the offer of orange juice or coffee, to a question from my row companion about my destination. I feel stronger, but not from fifteen minutes of sleep. From moving from my own sufficiency and strength—or lack thereof—to God's. I literally, physically feel strength flow into me. It is not caffeine induced. It is supernatural. I have gone from a wilted flower on a sunny stoop, to a tree strong and tall alongside a riverbank.

No physiological explanation accounts for the strengthening. I am in the midst of the miraculous.

Fifteen minutes of finding God as my resting place restored my soul. It doesn't substitute for laying down in green pastures, but I realize humbly how much God longs for me to rest in him. To find his sufficiency in my own weakness, his rest in my fatigue, his power in my severely compromised abilities to be in ministry.

Along with the strength comes an ability to love—as I turn to my seat companion and as I later hoist my luggage from baggage claim and greet my host for the weekend retreat.

Whether in an aluminum container flying through the sky or on a picnic blanket beside a rippling stream, our Shepherd delights to restore our soul when we relinquish the issues that separate us from him.

With God as our resting place, we can run with perseverance the race that is set before us. There will always be a race.

And there will always be a resting place.

Notes

Introduction

p. 13   "Henri Nouwen defined discipline as": Henri Nouwen, cited in "Moving from Solitude to Community to Ministry," *Leadership,* spring 1995, p. 81.

p. 14   Examen of consciousness and examen of conscience: Richard Foster, *Prayer: Finding the Heart's True Home* (New York: HarperCollins, 1992), pp. 27-28.

Chapter 2: The Famished Soul

p. 32   "Two-thirds of Americans are overweight": National Health and Nutrition Examination Survey (NHANES), as reported in "Sleep, Dog Help Weight Loss: Study," *Daily Jefferson County Union,* November 17, 2004, pp. 1, 8; Grant Pick, "Slim Chance: Even a Small Change in Habits Can Cut Obesity Down to Size, But Long-Term Successes Are Few," *Chicago Tribune Magazine,* April 25, 2004, p. 12.

pp. 32-33   Ruth Senter on God's desire: Ruth Senter, *Longing for Love: A Woman's Conversations with a Compassionate Heavenly Father* (Minneapolis: Bethany House, 1997), pp. 44-46.

Chapter 3: Abandonment and God

p. 46   "To be deserted by love": Ruth Senter, *Longing for Love: A Woman's Conversations with a Compassionate Heavenly Father* (Minneapolis: Bethany House, 1997), p. 51.

p. 48   "We either become alcoholics": Janet G. Woititz, *Guidelines for Support Groups: Adult Children of Alcoholics and Others Who Identify* (Pompano Beach, Fla.: Health Communications, 1983), pp. 11-12.

p. 49   "God's hiddenness can be expected": Richard J. Foster, *Prayer: Finding the Heart's True Home* (New York: HarperCollins, 1992), pp. 19-20.

p. 49   "When some of this solid, perfect food": John of the Cross, *Ascent of Mount Carmel* 2.7.5, quoted in *God Speaks in the Night: The Life, Times, and Teaching of St. John of the Cross* (Washington, D.C.: ICS Publications, 2000), p. 154.

Chapter 4: The Spotlight Self

p. 64   "We dress people up, put make-up on them": Editorial in *Christianity Today*, March 2, 1998, p. 14.

Chapter 5: Depression and Faith

p. 77   Twenty-five percent diagnosed as mentally ill: A psychiatrist quoted by Pam Kidd in *Daily Guideposts 1998* (Carmel, New York: Guideposts, 1997), p. 68.

p. 78   Fewer than half seek medical treatment: Tracy Thompson, *The Beast: Reckoning with Depression* (New York: G. P. Putnam, 1995), p. 280.

p. 81   "People who had a loved one die when they were young": Mary Ellen Copeland, *The Depression Workbook: A Guide for Living with Depression and Manic Depression* (Oakland, Calif.: New Harbinger, 1992), p. 19.

p. 81   "A dead weight of not-good-enoughness": Lewis Smedes, quoted by Sheila Walsh, *Honestly* (Grand Rapids: Zondervan, 1996), p. 85.

pp. 81-82 Some of shame's symptoms: An anonymous hospital psychologist quoted by Sheila Walsh, *Honestly*, pp. 92-93.

p. 82   "By this time, depression had taken over my brain": Thompson, *Beast*, p. 56.

p. 83   "He became cold, and he was convinced": "Martin Luther: The Later Years and Legacy," *Christian History*, Issue 39.

p. 84   Duke University psychologist's exercise regimen: Karen Springen, "The Serenity Workout," *Newsweek*, September 24, 2004, p. 68.

pp. 85-86 "My hope is build on nothing less": Edward Mote, "On Christ the Solid Rock," c. 1834.

p. 86   "Lord, take the dimness of my soul away": George Croly, "Spirit of God, Descend Upon My Heart," 1867.

Chapter 6: In the Maker's Mark

p. 93   Maxine Hancock's definition of creativity: Maxine Hancock, *Creative, Confident Children* (Old Tappan, N.J.: Fleming H. Revell, 1985), p. 122.

p. 95   "Creative talent is normally distributed": Alex Osborn, *Your Creative Power: How to Use Imagination* (New York: Charles Scribners', 1948), p. 17.

p. 96   "Any activity becomes creative": John Updike, *Picked Up Pieces*, as quoted in *Reader's Digest*, July 1998, p. 49.

p. 97   "Creativity 'arises out of the struggle'": Rollo May, quoted in Karen Mains, *Open Heart, Open Home* (Wheaton, Ill.: Mainstay Church Resources, 1998), p. 189.

p. 97   Karen Mains on creativity: Karen Mains, *Open Heart, Open Home* (Wheaton, Ill.: Mainstay Church Resources, 1998), p. 189.

p. 98   Creativity may "affect immune function, improve health": Ruth Richards, quoted in Nadia Zonis, "How to Be More Creative," *Ladies Home Journal*, November 1992, p. 106.

p. 100   "The most productive brainstorming meetings": Vatche Bartekian, "Learn to Be More Creative," AskMen.com <http://askmen.com/fashion/body_and_mind/9_better_living.html>.

Chapter 7: Holy Smokes

p. 108   Anger and higher mortality rates: Redford Williams, cited in Allison Glock, "Anger: How to Handle It," *Special Report*, July-August 1993, pp. 10-11.

p. 108   "People who regularly quashed their anger": Glock, "Anger," p. 9.

p. 112   "Which is more respectful": Michele Novotni and Randy Petersen, *Angry with God* (Colorado Springs: NavPress, 2001), p. 90.

Chapter 8: Get a Grip

p. 125   "We become stressed and anxious": Anonymous, *The Twelve Steps—A Way Out: A Working Guide for Adult Children of Alcoholic and Other Dysfunctional Families* (San Diego: Recovery, 1987), p. 44.

Chapter 9: Money Madness

p. 138   "With 600 million credit cards in circulation": *NBC Today*, January 3, 2005.

p. 138   "Household debt for the average family": Gary Belsky, "Win Your War Against Debt," *Money*, April 1996, p. 159.

p. 138   "With an estimated $800 billion owed": *NBC Today*, January 3, 2005.

p. 142   "The average donation by adults": George Barna, *How to Increase Giving in Your Church* (Ventura, Calif.: Regal Books, 1997), p. 20, quoted at *Generous Giving* <www.generousgiving.org/page.asp?sec=4&page=311>.

Chapter 10: The Happiness Quotient

p. 157   "Happy people tend to be healthier": Harry Lodge and Chris Crowley, authors of *Younger Next Year,* on *NBC Today,* January 3, 2005.

p. 158   "Regardless of your past experiences": Richard Carlson, *You Can Be Happy No Matter What: Five Principles for Keeping Life in Perspective* (Novato, Calif.: New World Library, 1999), p. 70.

p. 158   "Joy and laughter are the gifts of living": Henri J. M. Nouwen, *Here and Now: Living in the Spirit* (New York: Crossroad, 1994), p. 31.

About the Author

Known for her vulnerability, spiritual depth and humor, Jane Rubietta is a popular and frequent keynote speaker at events around the continent. Her other IVP books include *How to Keep the Pastor You Love* and *Grace Points: Growth and Guidance in Times of Change.* Jane has a degree in marketing and management from Indiana University, then attended Capernwray Bible School and Trinity Evangelical Divinity School.

Jane and her husband, Rich, have founded the not-for-profit Abounding Ministries, whose mission is to offer people a life-changing experience of God's love in Jesus Christ through music, writing, speaking and retreats in communities, schools and churches. For more information, contact

Jane Rubietta
Abounding Ministries
225 Bluff Avenue
Crystal Lake, IL 60030
847-223-4790
jrubietta@abounding.org
www.abounding.org

Bringing *Resting Place* closer to home:

If your church, women's ministry or special events coordinator is interested in considering Jane for a conference, retreat, banquet or training event, please contact her at the above address.

ALSO AVAILABLE

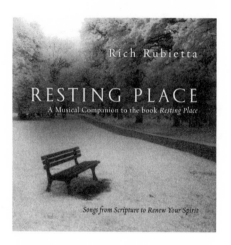

Rich Rubietta and Abounding Music offer twelve Scriptures set to music and surrounded by fresh lyrics to strengthen your walk with God. This CD serves as a companion to Jane Rubietta's book *Resting Place*.